DADDY
Bent-Legs

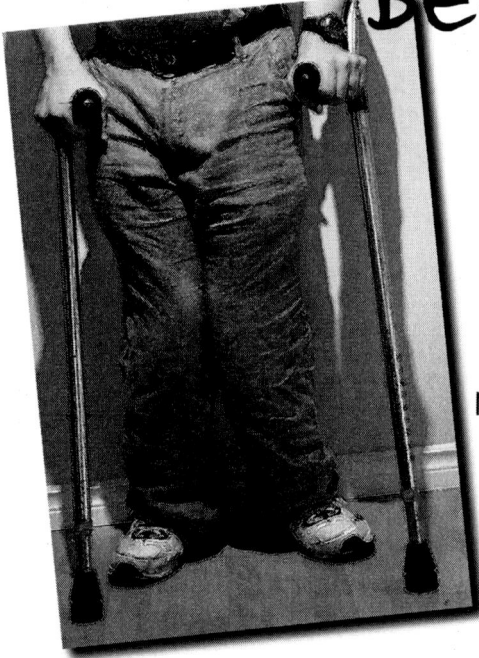

The 40-Year-Old Musings
of a Physically Disabled
Man, Husband, and Father

NEIL MATHESON

DADDY BENT-LEGS
The 40-Year-Old Musings of a Physically
Disabled Man, Husband, and Father

ISBN-10: 1-926676-35-1
ISBN-13: 978-1-926676-35-7

Printed in Canada.

Printed by Word Alive Press
131 Cordite Road, Winnipeg, MB R3W 1S1
www.wordalivepress.ca

WORD ALIVE PRESS
Just Write!

FOR ELANA A.

My encourager,
My teacher,
And my lover for life.

And thanks for the book's new title.
You were right, it is much better.

To my son, Jake.
Happy 1st Birthday!

To my mom, dad, and sister.
Thanks for giving me a normal life,
in spite of my disability.

foreword

*"Your word is a lamp to my feet
and a light for my path."*
(PSALM 119:105)

I suppose, technically, I didn't begin my Christian walk until about thirty-three years of age. Growing up, I only went to church three or four times a year. Everything I knew about God and Jesus was fairly superficial.

But still, it's weird. Despite my tremendous lack of exposure to all things Christian, my parents still raised both my sister and me to be Christian-like. I mean, I didn't go to church every Sunday, no. But, as a family, we did always go to at least one church service at both Christmas and Easter. Weddings and funerals, I learned, were God-infused, too.

Somehow, some way, I learned a little bit about God and the story of Jesus Christ. And I believed.

Of course, it isn't enough to just believe. I know that now; I didn't know it then.

My physical disability… my crutches… my bent legs: this was my test from God, I knew. And rather than growing up feeling bitter or shortchanged about everything, I welcomed the challenge. If this was to be my journey, so be it.

Thanks to strong parents (and a stable, normal family life), I grew up healthy. I liked my body; I liked myself.

By the time I hit thirty-three years of age, I really thought that I had it all figured out. But then, God surprised me. At thirty-three, I was transformed. Just when I thought that I knew myself pretty well, God delivered definitive proof to the contrary.

God knew me best; He had the better plan. And the proof came packaged in a way I did not expect...

table of contents

ODDS AND ENDS

FIRST, A LITTLE
BACKGROUND...

I wrote down some of my life experiences because I wanted to give others a glimpse into what it is like to be physically handicapped. I was born with mild Cerebral Palsy. Basically, it is just my legs that don't work quite right and I use a pair of elbow crutches to help me get around.

When I was about seven or eight, I transferred into a "normal" elementary school, Chaffey Burke. I remember how uncomfortable I was at first—scared that I wouldn't fit in with the other kids in Grade Two. I was the first physically handicapped student from G.F. Strong Rehabilitation Centre to make the jump into the regular school system. That was about thirty-five years ago. Back then, immersion of special needs students (e.g. either physically or mentally handicapped) was unheard of. G.F. Strong was full of kids just like me. There were kids on crutches or in wheelchairs who, as with me, had physiotherapy—routine exercise three times a day to help strengthen their bodies. But at Chaffey Burke, things were different. There were no crutches or wheelchairs. I was different.

Yet despite some early hardships over trying to fit in with the "normal" crowd and the regular school system, I never once wished that I was back at G.F. Strong. What needs to be said is that, from a very early age, I never felt like I "fit in" with the crowd at G.F. Strong, either. On the one hand, being surrounded by kids who were handicapped like me was comfortable. There is always comfort in the familiar. But on the other hand, I felt suffocated. G.F. Strong was more of a hospital than a school. Visits to the physiotherapist or with doctors were constant reminders of my handicap. Everyday, I was reminded that I was different. Every kid at G.F. Strong was different. We were all surrounded by peers who were different. Of course, in today's world of political correctness, being different is often celebrated. For me, though, I prefer to focus on similarities. That was true thirty-five years ago, and remains true today. Here, and throughout my autobiography, the word "different" carries a negative connotation. Thirty-five years back, most of the handicappers at G.F. Strong didn't seem to mind the "different versus normal" mentality. Personally, those labels struck me as being far too exclusive. I didn't want to be segregated. I didn't want to be pigeon-holed. I didn't want to be told that it was okay if I couldn't accomplish something, and that I shouldn't expect too much from myself. I didn't want to become accepting and complacent. I wanted to branch out. I wanted to expand my social horizons. I wanted to break free.

Yes, the first few years at Chaffey Burke were difficult. Yes, some kids would tease me and call me names. Yes, the teachers weren't convinced I'd be able to learn in a normal class at first. But the period of adjustment was, in fact, a small one and well worth the gamble.

Once I learned to relax, everybody else did too. I quickly learned to use humour as a tool to help ease awkward social situations and attract people's interest. Humour, I found, disarms people—makes them curious. And both students and teachers were more willing to approach me, get to know me, and ask questions if they saw me as someone familiar—as opposed to something strange or easily offended. Obviously, it is easy to fear, criticize, or tease something that is unknown or makes people uncomfortable. I learned that humour takes the edge off, and helps to equalize the playing field.

Throwing humour at situations is extremely effective. The odd joke or two can go a long way towards breaking the ice. I'm sometimes *over-reliant* on humour, it's true—using it as a defence mechanism to deflect hurt, for example. Nevertheless, I still believe that humour, used properly, will eventually conquer the hurt and win favour with others. Good humour can soften people and help dull sharp edges.

"YOU SHOULDN'T THROW STONES AT A GUY WHO HAS A PAIR OF STICKS"

I don't remember many of my experiences in elementary school, actually. Once I made it through that first year of transition from G.F. Strong to Chaffey Burke, the five years that followed were relatively normal. A few bits and pieces do stand out, though.

I recall one particular episode in Grade Seven, for instance. I remember the foul-mouthed jerk in my class whose idea of fun and recreation was to harass me during recess and lunch hour. After all, I was on crutches. To him, I was easy bait. At first, I put up with his verbal abuse. But one day, after two weeks of uninterrupted assault, I finally decided that enough was enough.

He was at it again.

"You're nothin' but a useless cripple!"

I said nothing, turned around, and started walking away.

He laughed at me and said, "Hey cripple! Where ya goin'?"

My crutches must have been magnetic. I couldn't get rid of the guy.

"Why do you always follow me around wherever I go?" I asked.

"Because."

"Because why?"

"Because I like to bother ya."

"Why?"

"'Cause you're a cripple."

After a few seconds of silence, I said, "Look, just leave me alone, okay?"

"No."

As usual, my diplomatic approach wasn't working. A few more seconds passed in silence.

"Listen, I could split your head open with one of these things," I said, raising a crutch.

Again, I had used this more violent tactic before. He knew it was an empty threat. I had never thought of my crutches as weapons, let alone pick a fight with anyone before, and I wasn't too eager to break with tradition.

"Ha! I could rip those crutches right off your arms before you even had a chance to swing at me. You'd be totally helpless without them, wouldn't you?"

I could think of nothing to say in reply but, nonetheless, I was pretty sure that this threat of his was just as empty as mine had been.

"Go ahead. Just try to hit me. I dare ya," he said.

In previous weeks, I had ignored this taunt of his. On this particular day, however, his invitation was very tempting. Still, I decided to give diplomacy another chance, and said,

"Just go away, okay?!"

"You gonna make me?"

"Yeah."

"Ha! I'd like to see you try."

"I'm warning you..." I said, raising a crutch.

It was right about then that he started laughing at me again. I couldn't believe it. He just stood there, laughing! Twenty seconds into his hysterics, I had heard enough, though. I swung my crutch at him in one quick, follow-through motion and it hit good and hard across his knees. His body folded up like a wet, two-ply Kleenex tissue and fell to the ground. He screamed in pain. Tears streamed down his face.

He was still lying on the ground when I walked away. And I felt good. A part of me did, at least. In any event, he never bothered me again after that.

STICKY PANTS

Now, don't get me wrong, shopping malls can be fun. I mean, I like going to shopping malls to people-watch, visit the music stores or computer shops, but all in all, I hate shopping. I hate the crowds. And if I find a good pair of jeans in a particular clothing store, I hate going into those stupid fitting rooms with cramped cubicles. In no time at all, I'm tired, overheated, my legs feel like tree stumps, my feet are all sore and prickly, and I want to go home. Over the years, based on personal experience, I have learned to associate shopping malls with supreme dullness and displeasure, and even the occasional disaster. Take the following example, for instance. Okay, ready? Go back about thirty years and picture this…

I am twelve years old, the January sales are on, and I am having my usual problem navigating a clear course through the mob.

"Slow down!" I yell, quickening my pace as I see my parents vanish in the sea of heads. Suddenly, my crutches give way. Unable to reverse the force of gravity, I fall to the floor.

"Are you all right, son?" asks one man, pulling me up by my left arm, almost tearing it off at the shoulder.

"Yeah. Yeah I'm fine," I say, first checking to see that my arm was still attached… then looking at a large, wet orange stain on my pants.

"Here's your sticks, son," he says.

"Thanks a lot."

"No problem."

Then I see my mom in a store across the way, waving her arms frantically trying to attract my attention.

"Where were you? We thought we'd lost you!"

"You did."

"You've got an orange stain on your pants."

"I know."

"What happened?"

"Nothing."

"What's with the orange stain?" my dad asks.

"I slid on a Slurpie."

"You okay?"

"Yeah."

"You sure?"

"Uh huh."

"Well, I guess there's no sense continuing this shopping spree in wet, sticky, orange pants, is there? Let's get on home."

The truth is that my dad hates shopping just as much as I do, and he saw this "Slurpie Incident" as the perfect escape. A happy coincidence. Something that would pry Mom away from all the stores, and cut our little outing short by at least two hours.

"How 'bout taking the escalator down?" my dad asks.

"Forget it! I'm never going down on one of those things again," I say.

Dad gives me that look of his, but I pretend not to notice and go off in search of an elevator.

Now, see, that look my dad gave me, the one I pretended not to notice… there's more to this story. About three weeks previous, I had another little "incident" that Dad was still teasing me about.

I was with my mom. She was helping me find Christmas gifts for Dad and my sister. We'd only been in the mall an hour and already my mom's arms were full of last-minute gift ideas.

"Let's go check out the bottom floor," she said, as we slowed to a stop in front of an escalator.

"Shouldn't we take the elevator?"

"It's way at the other end of the mall. This way will be quicker."

"It's just that with your arms full and all, I thought…"

"I'll still be able to hold on to you."

"With *what?*"

To this, my mom responded by hooking a single, solitary finger in one of the belt loops on the back of my pants.

"Now go," she said. End of discussion. I stood at the top of the escalator and looked down. No problem. All I had to do was synchronize my approach (well, perhaps "lunge" is most appropriate) so that both crutches hit a rapidly disappearing top stair at precisely the right time. Then it was a simple matter of a quick hop so that both legs hit the stair behind. Piece of cake. It was all routine. I waited to make my move. Crutches ready… Lunge! (Check.) Now the quick hop. Hop. Come on legs: hop! hop! (Mayday! Mayday! I am experiencing complete communication failure with legs…) Bail out! Bail out!

It was too late. By the time my legs had decided to join the rest of my body, my toes were precariously perched on a stair five steps up and to the rear, and my crutches were planted down on a stair way out in front of me. I was in a suspended nose-dive. And I could hear the belt loop ripping from my pants… I remember thinking, *Uh-oh… oh no… oh, God, help!*

It seemed like forever before I finally touched down (safely!) on the shiny white and level floor. I could see the judges holding up their score cards. For artistic impression: 5.2, 5.4, 5.2... only 4.8 from the Canadian judge. Figures. Next, the marks awarded for technical merit...

So to recap, then, in the space of about three weeks, I had slipped on a wet, sticky orange drink *and also* managed to almost kill myself trying to go down an escalator. Needless to say, looking back on everything, that wasn't one of my better months. To this day, I have yet to set foot on another escalator or buy myself an orange-flavoured Slurpie. The mere sight of either causes me to wince a bit. A stomach twitch. A mild fear.

CRAMPED CUBICLES

I used to go shopping for clothes with my mom all the time. As a young kid, I had very little say in the matter, after all. I love my mom, of course, but regardless, I hated shopping for clothes.

I liked getting new clothes; I just didn't like having to try them all on. It was too much work. It tired me out. My mom would go into a store, rummage through the racks, and within the first five minutes she'd already have a whole armload of stuff for me to try on. I would mount a mild protest but, in the end, such efforts were futile, I knew. Ultimately, all episodes ended with me trudging off to the fitting rooms in defeat.

I never went down without a fight, though. I always managed a sarcastic quip of some sort.

"Gee Mom, only six pair of pants and eight shirts... is that all you could find?!"

Although she'd never admit to it, I'm sure my sarcasm would tire her a little. A very small victory, but a victory nonetheless.

My victories were always short-lived, though. All too often, I'd make my way to a fitting room only to find that it was yet again too small. I hated cramped cubicles. And as if that weren't enough, most cubicles were rarely equipped with a chair or bench. Without crutches, my balance isn't all that great, so it really helps if I have something to sit on. I can stand to try on shirts, no problem. But trying on pants was a real chore. If I couldn't find anything to sit on, I was forced to sit on the floor. Not a big deal if the floor was clean, perhaps. Except that sometimes, the privacy curtains or doors didn't reach all the way to floor. Anyone walking past, therefore, would be treated to a showing of me in my underwear, flailing about like a wounded crab. Wonderful.

BEDPANS AND THE MILKSHAKE SOLUTION

G rade Eight was a busy year for me. See, I had to miss the last five months of school to recover from surgery. The doctors stretched my hamstrings so that I would stand straighter at the knees, and shifted some bone around in both feet so they wouldn't roll over on the inside arches as much when I walked. I remember...

I surveyed the hospital room and met the three guys I was sharing it with.

"Well, the surgery's tomorrow morning. Do you feel nervous about it or anything?" my mom asked.

"No. I think I'll be okay," I said.

I saw a strange-looking object sticking out under my bed.

"What's that?"

"It's a bedpan."

"A bed p—! You mean I'm supposed to take a dump in *that*?"

"I'm afraid so."

"Well, there's no way I'm using that thing!"

"You're going to be here for *five* days, Neil. Sooner or later you'll have to—"

"I'm not going to use it. Five bucks says I won't have to."

"And just how do you propose to do that?"

"I'll stick with the vanilla and chocolate milkshakes."

STILL IN THE
HOSPITAL

My parents and sister came to visit. As usual, the nurses had me loaded up on painkillers. A combo of morphine and valium.

My mom, noticing the untouched dinner tray, says, "Haven't you had anything to eat yet?"

"Yeah, a chocolate shake," I say.

"Is that all?"

"I wasn't hungry."

"Well, you've got to eat more. Are you still trying to hold out on using the bedpan?"

Absolutely. Nevertheless, I keep this little morsel of intelligence to myself. So instead, I say, "I haven't been hungry. Really. I think it's all the drugs they've been giving me."

That was mostly true, actually. I had answered her question quite honestly. Yet I could tell from the expression on my mom's face that it hadn't done much to ease her suspicions. Her lips were loosely pursed and I could tell from the small, oval-like shape of her mouth that she was poised to say something in protest. So I quickly jumped in, ahead of her mouth, to change the subject.

"When do I get to go home?" I asked.

"In a couple of days. The doctor told me that you'd be in the full-length casts for about fourteen weeks."

"What about the short ones?"

"Probably around another eight weeks or so."

"Holy!" my sister exclaimed, finally getting a word in.

Not to be outdone, my dad, in his best sarcastic tone, added, "Lots of fun, eh?"

"So how are you doing?" my sister asked.

"Pretty good, I guess."

"Here. This is for you," she says, handing me a home-made card... cut out of red paper, in the shape of a heart.

I opened the card. It read:

GET WELL SOON NIEL!
LOVE YOUR SISTER
BONNIE
XOXO

My name was spelled wrong. But it was a nice gesture, regardless. My sister has always been a bad speller; it's part of her charm. And truth be told, it's probably her most notice-able character flaw... which is to say, not a serious one and easily forgivable. Indeed, for a sister who was a full fifteen months older than me, Bonnie and I managed to have a pretty good relationship growing up. A few sibling squabbles, yes. But that's it.

Anyway, getting back to the hospital visit. This particular visit, on this particular day, wasn't all hugs and kisses. Despite the very nice heart-shaped card, something terrible happened. Something unbelievably painful. It was an innocent mistake. Such a little thing. A very little thing.

Bonnie nudged my bed, moving it ever-so-slightly. But that was enough. Pain shot through my body from toe to top. Real pain. Bad pain. Pain worthy of a loud scream. Except that I didn't have the energy to scream. Loaded up on drugs, I was too tired and weak. Instead, I just grit my teeth and turned many shades of white.

Needless to say, my sister was very apologetic. Soon after, my mom asked a nurse for more drugs.

RETURNING HOME
WITH PLASTER CASTS

A few days passed and I was at home once again in my own bed, a fortress of pillows. My mom would jam a bunch of pillows between the casts to keep my legs in an optimal and comfortable position. My granddad had bought a color TV with remote to put in my bedroom—and since I had to spend twenty-three and a half hours in bed every day, it was a good thing to have. I had a wheelchair, yes, but because my legs were covered in all that heavy plaster and unable to bend at the knee, sitting in the chair put a lot of strain on my lower back. After about ten minutes, I would have to pack it in. If I wasn't sleeping or playing cribbage with my mom or chess with my dad, the TV would keep me company. Even if I wasn't really watching it, I would leave it on. I watched a lot of Daytime television: *The Price Is Right*, old reruns of *Perry Mason*, talk shows… but that wasn't the worst of it. I actually got hooked on the soap operas. I was a Soap Junkie…

My sister peeked her head through the door of my room. "Hey, all right, *General Hospital*! Has it just started?"

"Yeah. Come on in."

"Do you need all these pillows?"

"No. Help yourself."

She propped a pillow behind her head and sprawled out on the bed beside me. This was our quality time together.

OFF WITH THE LONG,
ON WITH THE SHORT

Finally, after my legs had spent fourteen weeks in full-length plaster casts…

The doctor finished cutting my casts off. I looked at my legs. They were so thin. So wasted looking. So *yellow!* Dead skin. Gross. My legs were shaking. A lot. Like Jell-O trees in a gale force wind. And I couldn't stop them.

"Look at my legs. How come they're shaking so much?"

"Well, they haven't had any stimulation whatsoever for the last three months. They'll start to calm down after they get over that initial shock," the doctor said.

As soon as he finished washing the dead skin off my legs, the doctor began recasting them—slapping on fresh, wet plaster. These short ones wouldn't come off for another eight weeks. But in the meantime, the doctor said that I could start doing some exercises to strengthen the upper leg. And when the short casts came off, he said that I could go to work on my calf muscles. But the only thing I could think about as he was telling me all this was that, when I got these casts off, I wouldn't have to wear those big, metal leg braces with the ugly brown shoes ever again! I'd finally be able to wear plain, ordinary running shoes. And after I got these casts off, I'd also be able to have my first real bath in five months. Not just a simple sponge. I was glad of that, too.

BACK AT JUNIOR HIGH, POST-OP

I entered Grade Nine with straighter legs, wearing my first pair of plain ordinary running shoes. Fully recovered from surgery, I came back from a seven-month break, a super-extended summer vacation… to resume my alter ego: the reluctant adolescent student.

I really didn't like Junior High much. Much of what was taught I found boring and impractical. Especially algebra. Its logic and purpose was lost on me. Ninety-nine percent of the adolescent population shared this opinion, surely.

Despite a lack of enthusiasm for junior high, I made it through okay. I got all passing grades, survived my first bouts with acne, and even started liking girls. Looking back, I was a terrible flirt. We all were, really. What else was there? In my day, most adolescents were awkward and clumsy. Certainly not as streetwise as teenagers today.

Still, I got to be pretty cocky with girls who strolled down the hallway between classes or at lunch. I was especially smitten with two girls, in particular. I would sneak up from behind and, with my crutch extended, give the girls a sweet little innocent pat on the butt. Yes, I was pretty cool. The girls would turn around, see me, and flash a quick smile. We were all giggling flirts.

SENIOR HIGH, WITH GRADUATION LOOMING

I didn't start liking school again until I moved on to Senior High. Grades Eleven and Twelve were both fun. The classes were more interesting, the teachers better. Finally, I was learning about things that interested me, that challenged me. The school curriculum had value. Finally, I had some choice over which courses I wanted to take—a freedom sadly lacking in years previous. I loved English. Canadian History. Human Biology, most of all. I had some truly wonderful teachers. By the time Grade Twelve was half-complete, I had already started thinking about college and university. With graduation looming, I was ready to tackle the world.

I wasn't really in any kind of rush to leave high school, though. Grade Twelve was fun, life was easy, and there were plenty of other things that I had to tend to first. Like the Christmas Dance. I can boogie pretty good on my crutches, I think, but I have always liked the slow dances best. Hanging on to a girl for dear life, without crutches, hoping not to fall, hoping to avoid embarrassment. I called it "stick-less dancing." And despite my bit of fumbling, this was great entertainment, indeed.

OUR BEST FAMILY
VACATION, EVER

In Grade Twelve, during Spring Break, I went to Hawaii with the rest of my family. Hawaii was our first really exotic vacation together. Mom and Dad had been to Hawaii before, twice, but both times had been without me and my sister. In fact, the only times Bonnie and I had even been out of the province were on trips to Bellingham and Point Roberts. But now, here it was: I had two weeks off for Spring Break, and I was off to the islands of Oahu and Maui with Mom and Dad and Bonnie. And Mike. Back then, Mike was my sister's boyfriend of two years. Mike has moved up in the ranks since then, though, and is now her husband. Anyway, there we all were, on our way to Hawaii for twenty glorious days of sun and fun.

Even though I would end up missing six days of school, all of my teachers were very considerate. I didn't have many homework assignments to bring with me on the trip. My English Literature teacher wanted me to read Shakespeare's *Hamlet*, and my Creative Writing and Journalism teacher wanted me to keep a journal of my trip. And that's all.

What follows, is a relatively complete transcription of my travel log. Keep in mind that I was writing this journal for an English teacher. Knowing who my reading audience would be, then, I tried to write with as much creative flair as possible, as well as include a few really big words…

●●◆●●

March 6, 1987: We all got up at six o'clock this morning and were ready to leave for the airport by 7:30. The plane was forty minutes late. We didn't get off the ground until 10:30. This was my first time on a 747. The plane was jam-packed with seats and, given its exterior bigness, there was less leg room than I had expected. The service was great, though. I had the champagne breakfast, complete with omelette and steak. During the five-hour flight, I occupied myself with *Hamlet*.

When we finally touched down on the island of Oahu, the first thing I noticed stepping out of the plane was the heaviness of the air. It tickled my nose and throat. Feeling that first blast of hot, humid air blow up against your face is a bit of a shock, believe me. Anyway, looking around, the very next thing I noticed was the palm trees galore!

Next, we went through U.S. Customs, found all our luggage, picked up the rental car, and drove to The Outrigger Seaside Surf Hotel in Waikiki. The traffic here is terrible! Much of Oahu's highway system, it appears, consists of highways that are, for the most part, eight lanes wide—four lanes in each direction. In some places, there are two highways stacked one on top of each other. Also, I think my dad is overwhelmed with all the signs along the highway… the ones that show route numbers and give directions and such. A lot of the "go this way" signs, it seems, give directions which are either terribly ambiguous or, better yet, are placed only a few feet ahead of the spot where you have to turn off. My dad says that the signs are so bad he can't understand why they don't just have directions like, "If you want to get to Waikiki Beach, you should have turned left back there."

We all walked down to the Waikiki Public Market after dinner. It's only about a block away from our hotel. The market has to be seen to be believed. For starters, the market, which covers an area approximately equal to that of two football fields placed side by side, is located under an absolutely mammoth tree, called a banyan tree. I have never seen, let alone heard of this species of tree before, but apparently banyan trees are actually native to India, not the islands of Hawaii. The tree is an elaborate mess of thick roots, large trunks, and branches… a huge, gnarled, knotted organic blanket. Some of the trunks and roots are over thirty feet tall and spread outward, sometimes as far as fifty yards, before setting down in the soil again.

••◆••

March 7, 1987: Got up this morning and found my mom feeding some doves out on our balcony. Bran Flakes. The doves actually seemed to like the stuff. One thing's for sure, none of those doves will be suffering from constipation.

We all went to the beach this morning. The beach that we stopped off at was sheltered by a natural reef, so the water, as a result, was calm and quiet. The color of the water here is just amazing! The postcards don't lie, believe me. The ocean at this particular beach looked like crisp, liquid opal—or, if you prefer a simpler analogy, like Colgate gel toothpaste. Anyway, the water looked so inviting that I went in for a swim. The water was very warm, but it was also very salty! Just the smell of it made my nostrils tingle, and for that tiny bit which soaked through my lips, the taste was quite overpowering.

After the beach, we paid a visit to the zoo, had dinner, and then finished off the day by looking in all the stores that lined the street outside our hotel. I can't believe how warm it is out on the streets at 10:30 at night. Here it is, the beginning of March, and we're all walking around in shorts and t-shirts.

●●◆●●

March 8, 1987: Today, we all took off to the beach and I tackled the waves. I stood in the water with my crutches for the first little while, just until I got used to the wicked undertow that my dad warned me about. The churning water slammed into me and then heaved backward with tremendous force. The retreating waves, a.k.a. the undertow, ripped at my legs, but I had my crutches firmly planted and stayed standing. I ditched my crutches and plunked myself down in the waves after I was confident that I had a good feel for them. I sat in the churning water and attempted to bodysurf. It was right about then that the waves suddenly got worse. A lot worse. I only had time enough to hear my dad yell something like, "There's a big wave coming in right behind you, Neil!" before I was blindsided by a six-foot swell. The wave came crashing down on top of me and I was sucked under again as it retreated. I re-surfaced and caught a glimpse of my dad. The wave had knocked him flat on his butt and he was struggling to find his feet. Then another wave hit. And another. And another. I felt helpless. I was at the mercy of the waves. About all I could do was hold my breath, take quick gulps of air when I had the chance, and ride it out. I knew that as long as I kept holding my breath, I'd be okay. In other words, I wasn't in a state of panic, but at the same time, I wasn't having much fun either!

After what was probably no more than two minutes, though it seemed like much longer, the waves finally mellowed somewhat and I was able to crawl back up onto the beach. I kept crawling until I reached the top part of the beach, where the sand was hot and dry. And there I sat, victorious, and safe from even the most overzealous and rambunctious wave. Yet when it was all said and done, I had sand in my shorts and up my nose and my mom had to flush bits of sand from my eyes.

We have almost reached the end of another day and now, as I'm writing in my journal, I'm looking up into the mirror before me in the living room and I am rudely reminded that I, on top of everything else, have managed to get a little too much sun on my face as well.

●●◆●●

March 9, 1987: Today, we did the typical tourist thing and went to see the *USS Arizona* memorial at Pearl Harbour. The *USS Arizona* is a battleship that was sunk on that infamous day, December 7, 1941. The memorial basically consists of a simple platform structure built right out on the water, and the platform actually straddles over top of the sunken ship. The battleship is still relatively intact, with its gun turrets barely visible, protruding just above the waterline.

●●◆●●

March 10, 1987: We all saw some pretty spectacular shows at Sealife Park today. The National High Diving Champions were up first. The killer whale show was next. Then the dolphins. I love dolphins—they're so cool! I saw a few dolphins in a small holding pool. They were so close, yet I couldn't quite touch them, so I had to settle for a few giant sea turtles instead—they enjoyed a friendly pat or two.

After the sea turtles, Bonnie and Mike and I each threw a few fish to the sea lions. See, there's this place where you can buy fish for a buck apiece, and then walk up onto this small bridge, lean over the railing, and finally drop your fish into the mouths of hungry sea lions waiting below. One sea lion in particular, quite a bit smaller than all the others, looked so sad. I felt so sorry for him that I threw my first fish in his direction. The fish dropped right into his mouth, but at that very moment, this other big pig of a sea lion, which I immediately identified as "The Boss," stole the fish from the little guy's mouth before he had a chance to eat it. Undaunted, I threw another fish to the sad-eyed sea lion. Again, the fish dropped right into the little guy's mouth, and again "The Boss" stole it away from him. So there I am, down to my third and final fish, and the little guy looks up at me with those big, sad eyes. So of course, I throw down my last fish and it hit the little guy square on the snout and bounced off. The little guy hadn't even bothered to open his mouth when the fish fell down to him. Worse yet, when "The Boss" swam over to retrieve this fish, the little guy didn't even put up a fight.

I still haven't decided which of those two sea lions frustrated me the most.

●●◆●●

March 11, 1987: Today, we all hopped in the car and stopped off at a place called Hanama Bay to do some snorkelling. I saw hundreds of beautiful fish—all different sizes, shapes, and colors. It was like seeing a rainbow in chaos. I actually fed the fish, too. We used small chunks of white bread. We were told that bread is a good, safe food to give them. The fish like it. As soon as I held out a piece of bread, I would have a swarm of fish all around me. I liked it when a whole horde of them would brush up against my body, in pursuit of the bread. It was a wonderful sensation! I tickled all over.

●●◆●●

March 12, 1987: Today, we completed the entire driving circuit of Oahu. The less populated areas of the island are dry, barren, dirty slums... quite a contrast to all the rest!

After our sightseeing tour, we divided up. Bonnie and Mike spent a quiet evening by themselves to celebrate their second year of courtship, while Mom and Dad and I went to The Blue Dolphin for dinner. The Blue Dolphin is a very luxurious restaurant. Dad and I gorged ourselves on all-you-can-eat king crab legs. During dinner, we chatted with an Oregon couple that sat at a table beside us. The husband was especially entertaining...

"Boy, those crab legs sure look good!" the man said, looking over at my dad's plate.

The man's mouth was drooling with envy. Yet his comic tone was obvious. He wanted a few of our crab legs for himself, but was clever enough not to ask for them outright. My dad sensed the man's playful intentions and pushed the fun a little further.

"Mmmmm, yes. These crab legs are *sooo* succulent!" my dad crooned, pretending to be in absolute rapture over them.

The comedian from Oregon wasn't about to be upstaged. Casting his eyes on my dad's plate, the man barked like a dog. He even started to pant and whine.

This display amused my dad.

He patted the man's head and added, "Down, boy. Down! Good dog...!"

Then my dad tossed a couple of crab legs on the man's plate, and the man gave a bark of approval in return. The man ate his bounty and started the dog routine all over again. I tossed a couple more morsels on his plate. After all, any guy crazy enough to bark for food deserves a certain degree of respect. Besides, I wanted to shut the guy up.

●●◆●●

March 13, 1987: Well, here it is, the end of another day. Right now, I'm sitting out on the balcony of our seventh-floor hotel suite… watching the sun set. The sunsets here are truly breathtaking. I enjoy them so much that, in the eight days we've been here, I've made a special point of seeing each and every one. Aside from the sunsets, I also continue to be amazed at the astounding number of high-rise hotels here. I look out at the horizon and all I can see, besides the sunset, is a crush of elongated rectangles.

●●◈●●

March 15, 1987: Yesterday morning, we all boarded a 737 to the island of Maui. After we landed, we picked up another rental car and drove to this resort called The Maui Eldorado, in Kanepoli. This will be our home for the next couple of days. The resort consists of several units, and our unit is almost as big as our house in Vancouver! Very luxurious, indeed…

Today, my dad and sister and I went up in a helicopter—our first time! Three other tourists who we had never met before also came along for the ride. My sister got to sit up front with the pilot, and Dad and I sat in the back with the other three. Everybody was seated forward and thus able to see out the front and side windows. Also, each one of us had a headset, so we could talk amongst ourselves with ease. Not only could we all hear and respond to each other, we could also listen and respond to the pilot while he directed our attention to the many different landmarks around the island. Of course, my sister asked the pilot about sharks and the probability of a shark attack when swimming along the island beaches. I wonder how many other people would think to ask a fully-certified helicopter pilot that!

For some reason, I thought that this helicopter ride would feel quite a bit different from a ride in a plane. I expected that I would feel a lot more motion in a helicopter, as opposed to the gentle bumps that you occasionally get on a plane. As it turned out, the helicopter ride was very smooth. In fact, it was even smoother than a car traveling along a newly paved highway. Even when the pilot would yank the helicopter into a really sharp, steeply banked turn, I couldn't feel the least bit of motion.

The helicopter trip lasted for about an hour and a half, and we got an exciting bird's-eye view of the island. We even flew right down into the crater of a dormant volcano! The surface of this crater looked as if ten thousand marshmallows had melted, and then hardened into a mass of miniature peaks and valleys... yes, the entire surface of this crater had a very distinctive "toasted marshmallow," "puffy, fluffy" look to it... Anyway, we saw lots of other things, too. For instance, we saw at least seven waterfalls—and they're especially spect-acular, I think, when you can see each one from way up in the sky, like we did... because that way, you get to see the whole thing. Aerial views of agricultural land are also neat because only then can you see just how intricately planned everything is. There are crops of pineapples, for instance, planted row upon row... and the whole mess of them create wonderfully elaborate geometric shapes.

●●◆●●

March 16, 1987: This morning, we all decided to go down to the swimming pool. Actually, I was a little slow to get out of bed this morning so Mom, Dad, Bonnie, and Mike left without me. They did, however, promise to reserve a slab of cement for me.

A little later, I was finally ready. I grabbed my towel and suntan lotion and started out for the pool. Partway down, I intercepted a man on the walking path...

"Morning. Where are you off to?" the man asked.

"The pool."

"Whatcha gonna do down there?"

Now was that a stupid question, or what? Not wanting to seem impolite, though, I answered it nonetheless.

"Swim," I said.

"You can swim!"

"Uh-huh."

"With those?"

"Well, no, I don't actually wear my crutches while I'm swimming."

"Oh."

And with that, the man walked off. I get the feeling I hadn't satisfied very many of his curiosities. As he left, I could see from the expression on his face that he was even more perplexed than ever.

●●◈●●

March 17, 1987: One quick note: this is our last day at the Eldorado. We'll be packing our bags later this afternoon, getting into the car, and driving around to the other side of the island, to a place called Kehei, where we'll be booking into another hotel.

●●◈●●

March 19, 1987: Well, here we are, at a hotel called The Halekai O'Kehei... it's got shuffleboard, a miniature golf course, and everything!

31

We went to the beach today and rode the waves on these pieces of stiff rubber called Boogie Boards. The boards are rectangular in shape and, basically, all you have to do is get in the water, place this thing under your belly, paddle out, wait for a good wave... and go! But then again, when you actually get out on the waves, staying nicely secure on your Boogie Board is sometimes difficult, if not impossible. It's a wonder I didn't wreck my back, really. This one time, I paddled out and got sideways on a six-foot swell. The wave rolled me up and spit me out and crunched my body on the high and dry...

We've been sighting lots of whales from our balcony overlooking the ocean... occasionally we'll see one jump right out of the water. Also, I have actually heard the whales while snorkelling right along the shore! At first, I was sort of freaked out, because I could hear these whistles, whines, and whimpers so clearly. I knew right away that these strange sounds were coming from whales—and I knew that these whales were probably a mile off shore—but at the same time, this beautiful, yet eerie "whale talk" was so loud and, as I said, I could hear it so clearly, that I half expected to see an enormous mass of blubber staring me right in the face. I had no idea that the sound waves from this "whale talk" could travel so well through the water!

●●◆●●

March 23, 1987: It has been very relaxing here at the Halekai O'Kehei. We haven't been doing much sightseeing. Instead, we've spent these last few days just sunning on the beach, mostly. And, as I sit here now, I can't help but face the reality that this vacation is about to end soon. Too soon. Just three more days...

Today, we all went out onto the deep, deep ocean (in a rather large, open-air boat), to see some humpback whales "up close and personal," as a television interviewer might say. We saw tons of whales (excuse the pun)! Humpback whales are such impressive creatures. I regard them as being very much like guardians... not only of the sea, but of the rest of our planet as well. There's something very mysterious and spiritual about these huge, majestic mammals... I realize what I have just written might seem a little weird, but nonetheless, I really believe that.

Anyway, as I was saying, we saw lots of these humpback whales. Apparently, all boats, even whale-watching vessels, are required by law to stay at least fifty yards back from an approaching pod of whales... yet, at the same time, should any of these wondrous creatures desire a closer look at us humans, they can "volunteer" to do so. As it turned out, many of the whales were curious and did, indeed, volunteer to approach our boat. Quite a few surfaced right alongside us. In fact, at times they were so close that I could almost touch them when I leaned over the ship's guardrails. I'm not kidding. And whenever the whales got up close like that, I got a really good look at them... especially when they rolled over on one side and raised their heads out of the water. As you probably already know, humpback whales do not have teeth. Instead, a humpback has hundreds of thin plates, called "baleens," which hang from its upper jaw. The whale uses these to filter out food from the water. Of course, I've seen pictures of humpback whales in books, but this is the first time I've seen them for real... and the baleen, I thought, looked very much like a huge, fine-toothed comb which had been wedged horizontally into the whale's mouth. The front, or snout of the whale, slowly tapered up into what seemed to me to be a giant, warted dill pickle... and the back of the whale, of course, tapered off into a big, long, shovel-like tail, called a "fluke." Such magnificent creatures, whales!

After we had visited with the whales for well over an hour, the time came to say goodbye. And the whales must have sensed this, I think... because as soon as the captain started turning the boat around, a large pod of them surfaced all around us to say their final goodbyes. Each of these whales actually waved farewell, or so appeared, with a gentle bend from fluke or fin.

●●◆●●

March 25, 1987: "Happy Birthday to me, Happy Birthday to me..."

I'm nineteen today. Nineteen is the age of official adulthood. Old enough to vote, and old enough to drink. At least, in my part of Canada. Here in Hawaii, the drinking age is twenty-one, so I'll have to save my drunken celebrations for when I return home.

Today is our last day of vacation. We fly home to Vancouver, and rain, tomorrow. With the five-hour flight, we should make it back around 12:30 in the morning. It'll be nice to get back home, I guess. I'm sure our dog is lonely. But, all the same, I wish we had another three weeks here.

We're all going to an outdoor luau later this afternoon to celebrate our last night... and my birthday, of course! From what my dad's told me, a luau is a big party where we, and about two hundred other guests, all sit around eating roast pig. There's singing, and dancing hula girls, too.

A SPECTRUM
OF SMILES

I used to have a poster of me hanging on my bedroom wall. And no, I'm not conceited or "stuck up." Give me a chance to explain.

It's an Easter Seals poster and I was the boy chosen for the "Help Easter Seals, Help Crippled Children" campaign in 1980. I was twelve years old at the time. On the poster itself are five black and white pictures of me set against a beige background. I am wearing the same thing in each picture: a white, button down shirt with brown horizontal and vertical stripes, a pair of dark brown cords, and brown shoes. My dirty blonde hair (or light brown, perhaps?) is cut long over the ears and parted on the left side of my head. I remember how terribly self-conscious I used to be about my ears. I thought they were ugly. I don't know why.

Anyway, so there I am, just standing there (all five of me), standing, I should say, with the aid of an old beat-up pair of crutches. All five of me smiling, buck teeth and all. My mom, who coerced me into braces the following year, used to affectionately refer to them as rabbit teeth. So for the next four years, not only did I have braces on my legs, but I had "railroad tracks" on my teeth as well. Kids at school would come up and ask me how much longer I had to wear braces, and I would say, "Which ones?"

Back to the poster. As I was saying, this rather large poster was composed of five separate photographs. Three pictures had me walking towards the camera. The third, middle photo was the largest. The last two pictures had me walking away, with an over-the-shoulder glance. The poster is essentially a spectrum of smiles, an overdose of cuteness. And if that was the effect the photographer had wanted to achieve, then I guess she was successful. I can only assume that she did, indeed, desire the "cuteness overdose"... because she did, after all, have over two hundred other pictures of me to choose from. I remember posing for all of those pictures, too. I twirled about like a real fashion model. And I must admit, it was lots of fun.

So why have this poster hanging on my bedroom wall? Well, did I mention the slogan printed across the top in big, bold green letters? "Help Easter Seals, Help Crippled Children." Crippled. I hate that word. I always have, even at age twelve. I used to hear that word quite a bit. Thirty years ago, it was a perfectly accepted word. It still is for some people, I guess, and it can be found in any English dictionary. Personally, I always took that word as an insult. Crippled. Just the sound of it is hideous. Crippled. Yuck! Yet here I am (all five of me) on a poster with "Help Easter Seals, Help Crippled Children" emblazoned above my head. I was okay with the terms *disabled* or *handicapped*, but I really hated the word *cripple*. Yet my own smiling face endorsed the message. I was endorsing an image. An image of cuteness.

It all started with a letter. A few physiotherapists at G.F. Strong Rehabilitation Centre convinced me to write to city planners and inform them of some difficulties I had to face in accessing public buildings. Buildings could be made more accessible to the physically handicapped in many ways. I included suggestions like installing elevators in all new schools. In older schools, where elevator installation wasn't possible, wheelchair ramps could be built instead. I also suggested that changing rooms in clothing stores be larger and equipped with chairs or benches, and that turnstiles in food marts and movie theatres be removed (my crutches were always getting caught in those things). My mom said that I should also include a little of my life history, along with my interests and hobbies. So I did. I wrote about Easter Seals' Camp Squamish, and how much fun I had there every year. I also wrote about my enjoyable times at the stables of The Handicapped Horseback Riders Association.

G.F. Strong and Easter Seals liked my letter so much that they decided to use it in a new campaign. I was chosen to be the poster boy. When the poster was ready to be plastered in every store window in the city and around the province, Easter Seals would (so they said) send a copy of my letter to every household as well. And they did. Only it wasn't the letter I had originally written. Not really. Easter Seals edited out my concerns over public building accessibility entirely. My comments on camp and horseback riding were the only two things left intact.

That 1980 poster and letter were part of the most successful campaign Easter Seals ever had. And it ran for the next three years.

Now, some thirty years later, I think about that poster and I have to laugh. That goofy smile tells it all. I had my fun writing letters and appearing on posters, but I really didn't change anything.

Still, I was only twelve years old at the time, right? How could I expect Easter Seals to take my concerns over building accessibility seriously? Or to have the public take me seriously! It shouldn't have surprised me that Easter Seals had grossly edited my letter. But it did. And thirty years ago, *crippled* was a totally acceptable term to use in reference to handicapped persons. So I had no reason to take offence to the word. But I did.

What I learned most from my experience of being a poster boy was that Easter Seals had pulled off a very cheap sell. In the end, they packaged up a cute face and presented it to the public. I was reduced to an image: a static, non-vocal, and cute image on a poster. The public took it from there.

FRAGMENTS

I think about that Easter Seals poster and I remember a lot of things. I remember myself at twelve years old, yes, but I also remember my years before then. I recall bits and pieces. Fragments of memories.

I remember the first operation on my feet when I was five years old. I don't recall those moments of the actual surgery, of course, but I do remember my stay in a hospital bed. I had a roommate, a boy about my age. Having a playmate was great. We shared our toys. I had a Snoopy hand puppet and a few Sesame Street finger puppets, and my roommate had a couple more.

I forget the exact time of curfew on our hospital ward, but I recall the nurse coming into our room every night to turn out all the lights. As soon as the nurse left, though, we would turn the lights on again. We always wanted to stay up late with our puppets.

The nurse would come in again. The lights would go out again. The nurse would leave. And the lights would go on. The cycle would repeat itself several times before my roommate and I grew tired of the nurse and fell asleep.

●●◆●●

I remember my friend Ernie from G.F. Strong. He and I were the best of buddies, and we remain good friends to this day.

We used to have races down the long halls of the center. And sometimes during a race, our crutches would tangle with one another in the heat of competition. Or better still, one of us would get our own two feet tangled up. Either way, bodies would frequently be catapulted and smashed to the hard floor. Bruises and scrapes and bloodied chins amidst laughter were not uncommon. The hilarity of it all did not escape us. The bigger the fall, the funnier it was. Why was the risk of injury fun? I don't know. Perhaps it was because we knew that with each race, with each tangle, and with each spill, we had tempted fate and survived. A victory worthy of a smile, at the very least.

●●◆●●

I remember the doctors that always wanted me to get x-rays taken of one bone or another. Honestly, I had so many x-rays as a child, it's a wonder I don't glow in the dark now. And as if x-rays weren't enough, I remember the semi-annual meetings for "formal physical assessments," where I was thoroughly examined in front of a panel of eight doctors. All my bones were poked and prodded: legs, feet, hips, and spine. When asked to walk to the end of the hall and back on crutches, I did. Several times. A few doctors would then speak in hushed tones amongst themselves, yet they were never very discreet… never quiet enough. I could hear them talking about me, the patient. My own family doctor was the only one who would address questions to me, and not my mom. The only one to address me by name. The rest of them were strange and uncomfortable.

●●◆●●

I remember my early years at Chaffey Burke Elementary School. I remember Grade Four. By then, I was well into my third year there and fully adjusted to a normal school environment. Yet having someone like me, a child with a disability, learning and participating in a regular classroom... this was big news. Thirty-five years ago, taking the leap from a rehabilitation centre to a typical, everyday elementary school was very rare indeed. At the time, most kids that were different attended "Special-Ed" classes and were integrated slowly. My integration, on the other hand, was decidedly more reckless. A headfirst plunge, sink or swim.

Anyway, one day in Grade Four, I became somewhat of an instant celebrity. I had camera crews from a popular, local TV show following me around for the day. All my classmates thought it was pretty cool. And it was. Sitting at my desk, a huge lens propped mere inches from my face, the camera man zoomed in even tighter for a few really extreme close-ups. A full-frame view of my eyeball, a nostril, an earlobe.

●●◆●●

Most of Grade Five wasn't that great. At a doctor's request, I had to go from my short, metal leg braces back into full-length leg braces. Whereas the short braces stopped below the knee, these longer ones locked both knees firm, and went from the ankles to the top of my hips. Even the big ugly brown boots themselves were five pounds heavier apiece. The braces were so heavy that I couldn't even lift my legs when I walked, and my toes would scuff against the ground. With the shorter braces, my legs had freedom to move and flex. In the full-length braces, movement was impossible.

This new lack of freedom was obviously quite a blow for me. I couldn't do everything as before. I couldn't play soccer with my classmates at lunch. With the short braces, I could. I could move a lot faster, stretch a lot further. I didn't kick the ball with a leg; I used my crutch. And I was a pretty good defender in front of goal. With an attacker charging in on net, I could swipe in quick with the long reach of a crutch to dislodge the ball from oncoming feet. Either that, or I would miss the ball entirely, and smack my crutch against oncoming ankles. My hobbling tactics were purely accidental, of course… but still, everyone wanted to have me on their team. I was a secret weapon.

So when I discovered that I could no longer play soccer, I became depressed. And when I realized my walking speed had slowed to a turtle-crawl, I became bitter. Here I was, age ten, already experiencing a mid-life crisis. It was fitting in many respects, since I often felt wise beyond my years, anyway. But it was tough, no doubt about it. I would cry myself to sleep some nights.

It took me a while, but eventually I realized that I didn't like being miserable. So I recomposed myself and moved along… perhaps a little slower, but nonetheless determined. Thankfully, life didn't sit still. And I went back into shorter, below-the-knee braces the following year.

I'M NO EXPERT

I always chuckle to myself at the people who assume that I'm an "expert" in all issues facing physically handicapped persons, just because I happen to have a physical handicap myself. Seriously, some people look to me like I'm a walking Encyclopedia of Handicapism. Truth be known, of all the handicapped individuals across North America, I'm probably the biggest "non-expert" there is. Everything I know about my Cerebral Palsy, for example, can be put on a piece of paper equivalent to the size of a very small napkin:

"My Cerebral Palsy is, in essence,
the product of 'a blood war' which took place
a little over forty years back, at birth.
My mom and dad's blood types were
very incompatible together…
It was this incompatibility which
damaged a tiny part of my brain…
and as a result, I was born
into this world with legs that
worked a little less than perfect."

So, that's about all I know. And that's about all I care to know, too. I couldn't be bothered with all the finite details. Leave all that medical mumbo-jumbo and technical jargon for someone else, thanks.

BONNIE AND
THE CHAIR

I had a wheelchair until I was about eight years old. I was still able to get around on crutches back then, but my parents would put me in the wheelchair whenever we went out for all-day excursions through the park, and things like that. It was a lot easier for my mom, dad, or sister to push me around in a chair than it was for them to stop every five minutes, waiting for me (and my crutches) to catch up. I didn't like having to use the wheelchair, though, because I was absolutely useless at manoeuvring it by myself. I don't know whether my arms were too short, too weak, or what, but I always had a heck of a time getting the chair to move any faster than a three-legged tortoise.

My sister always offered to get in behind the chair and push… and when she did, her legs pushed as hard and as fast as they could go. Bonnie used to take me out for "cruises" around the block all the time, just me and her, and every once in a while, she would push me up a really steep hill, turn the chair around, and release me… and the chair and I would be sent screaming down the hill. Bonnie, of course, would run after the chair, laughing. And by the time she caught up with me at the bottom of the street, I was laughing, too.

"UH, COULD YOU REPHRASE THAT, PLEASE?"

"So, what's wrong with you?"

I used to get that question a lot when I was growing up. I still do, occasionally. Not nearly as often as thirty or thirty-five years back, but yes, every few months or so, I'm bound to run into someone who asks me that. It sometimes happens while I'm riding the bus. Or sometimes someone will stop me as I'm walking down the street, or through a shopping mall, or a grocery store. Or waiting for an elevator.

It's a weird question, though. If it were me asking a question like that, I'm pretty sure I'd have the sense to rephrase it a little. Of course, people don't mean to offend, I know that. Indeed, most people are simply trying to make an attempt at polite conversation. To be friendly. And there's absolutely nothing wrong with that.

Still, it amazes me how that question, those exact words, tumble out of people's mouths. This awkward phrase is uttered mostly by adults, not children. No, young children don't ask vague questions. They are a lot more direct. Kids ask things like, "Why do you have to walk with those sticks?" Generally speaking, younger children do not offend with the way they ask questions.

But when an adult asks what's wrong with me? How am I supposed to answer that? Hmmm, let's see, what's wrong with me? Uh, let me think.

I'm always tempted to turn the question around, like:

"What's wrong with me? Nothing, I'm fine. Why, what's wrong with *you*?"

But as I said, I know most people aren't trying to offend me, so I do my best not to offend them. I'll usually say something simple and to-the-point:

"I was born with Cerebral Palsy."

A few people will reply back with, "Oh, I'm so sorry!"

Responses like that really bug me. I mean, what's to be sorry about? I was born with my disability. I'm used to it, and I've had a lot of years of practice. I have managed to get through life pretty well, thanks. So please, don't feel sorry for me.

The odd time—on very, very rare occasions—it is plainly obvious that the person asking that first awkward question of *"What's wrong with you?"* isn't showing a legitimate curiosity; sometimes people ask that question and don't really care to know the answer. Sometimes, the insincerity and rudeness sticks out and is easy to spot.

And I don't really feel like giving an honest answer to people who honestly don't care. Instead, I say something back like:

"Oh, it's because I drank far too much coffee as a young kid…"

The way I see it, sometimes an insincere question deserves an insincere response.

People lucky enough to hear my stupid one-liner about drinking too much coffee are suddenly instantly quiet. A tit-for-tat moment of realization for them—hopefully at least—that stupid is as Stupid does.

Genuine rudeness is rude; it's as simple as that.

A DEFINITION
OF ATTITUDES

CURMUDGEON: "An ill-tempered person
full of resentment and stubborn notions."
(WWW.THEFREEDICTIONARY.COM)

Fifteen years ago or thereabouts, someone gave me a small desk calendar, called *The Curmudgeon Calendar* that had various cankerous quotes from famous people, actors, or politicians. It was a daily calendar with a fresh quote for every day of the week. Out of all 365 quotes, one in particular immediately resonated with me in a big way as soon as I stumbled upon it:

"Whatever women do they must do twice
as well as men to be thought half as good.
Luckily, this is not difficult."
—CHARLOTTE WHITTON

●●◈●●

Of course, I had absolutely no idea who this Charlotte Whitton person was. And at first, I wasn't even sure why I was so intrigued with this memorable quote. After some quick research, I discovered that Ms. Whitton was essentially one of Canada's earliest feminists. Born in 1896, Whitton served as Mayor of Ottawa from 1950 to 1963. Before that, she was a lecturer, freelance writer, author, and all-around social activist.

Anyway, enough talk of important Canadian historical figures. I need to explain why Whitton's quote has somehow managed to stick in my brain for a full fifteen years! It took me a while to pinpoint this, but eventually I came upon the realization that Ms. Whitton's inspired feminist rant had distinct parallels with me, and others navigating through life with a physical disability. Whitton's quote illuminates the mindset of the many who struggle daily (be it big or small) with having to be forever labelled as living amongst a visible minority.

Based on my own personal experience, I most definitely felt an overwhelming need to continually prove myself worthy amongst the able-bodied crowd. My physical disability could never be seen as a weakness, I wouldn't allow it—and as a result, I was always pushing myself harder, reaching further. From a very early age, I somehow knew that I would have to work harder, or smile brighter, if I were to ever hope to achieve a relative equality amongst the able-bodied.

That need to constantly prove myself stuck with me until I reached my early thirties. At 30-plus years of life, I resigned myself to the notion that I had finally earned enough wisdom and experience to relax a little.

I have now come to an enlightened realization that I don't need to strive for accolades or special recognition in my daily life anymore—whether it be in the workplace, or even amongst family and friends. Don't get me wrong, hard work is still important. But oftentimes, being simply competent is enough. Giving myself the freedom to just be me, instead of struggling for every last inch on the battlefield—this is perhaps my most significant revelation over this last decade of a blessed life.

HUMOUR ME

In walking through life on bent legs, humour is the crutch I have relied upon most.

For me, humour works. If I'm meeting people for the first time, like going to a job interview, it's important for me to put everyone at ease. Make everybody feel comfortable about my crutches and me.

I don't necessarily have to address my handicap full-on. A roundabout way works just as well. I turn on the charm. I show people that I'm relaxed, that I'm a fun person.

I've been relying on humour for so long now that I don't even have to work at it. And that's good. Because like any good comedian or performer will tell you, it's important to be "on" and alert at all times. Of course, everyone has bad days. Some days, having to deal with my disability just plain sucks. But nonetheless, as a physically handicapped person, I've always felt added pressure to be a bit of a role model to others. And I don't really mind that. Not much, anyway.

Like it or not, physical appearance and first impressions are important. If people are going to judge me, I want to be sure to have my best foot forward at all times. Yes, people are going to notice my crutches and bent legs. That's unavoidable. But still, having the right attitude matters.

Growing up with a physical handicap, I was careful never to give anyone an excuse not to like me. I rarely complained or showed moodiness, even though there were plenty of times when I wanted to. For better or for worse, being able to project a positive attitude (even when you don't feel like it) is crucial. I am living proof that with a more positive outlook people can, and do, start to overlook crutches or wheelchairs.

ALL-WEATHER CRUTCHES

The only times I occasionally have difficulty getting around on my crutches are when it snows a lot. Most of the time, I don't have too much trouble in snow, especially when it's the dry, powdery stuff. Sure, dry snow can be slippery, too, but by shuffling my feet and using my crutches as ski poles, I usually avoid taking nasty falls. With heavier snowfalls, however, about all I can do is plough through the white stuff and hope for the best.

Despite the difficulties, though, I like snow. For me, autumn poses the greater hazard. First, the leaves fall off the trees. Then it rains, and eventually, the leaves on the ground decompose into a slippery brown sludge. It's like trying to walk on motor oil.

I LUV MY LEGS

I sometimes wonder what it would feel like to be able to walk with straight legs. I sometimes wish that I could be given the opportunity to experience the sensation of walking without the use of elbow crutches, for when I walk without crutches I feel like I'm going to fall over all the time. And occasionally I do fall. How strange it would feel to have straight legs, and be perfectly balanced!

Yet if someone were to ask me if I have ever felt like I had been cheated out of being able to do things like run, skip rope, jump fences, and climb trees, I would honestly answer no. Don't get me wrong: a big part of me would love to have the chance to experience an able body. Still, I don't really ever miss not having perfectly functioning legs because, well, I never had them to begin with. Aside from all that, though, I like the person I am. I am very content with the body and life I was given. Growing up, I felt lucky; I felt blessed, acutely aware, always, that my disability could have been so much worse… and that my life could have been a whole lot less fortunate, too.

In the grand scheme of things, a couple of bent legs are nothing, really. I have two eyes, two ears, two arms, and two legs to walk on, and that's good enough for me.

PHYSICAL DISABILITY
AND THE GAME OF GOLF

Vancouver, British Columbia has had its share of home-grown super stars. Michael J. Fox, Pamela Anderson, NBA stand-out Steve Nash, NHLer Paul Kariya, and singer/songwriters Bryan Adams and Sarah McLachlan are a few personalities that readily spring to mind.

And yet, despite all of that star power, our province—and maybe even the entirety of Canada—has only ever given birth to one or two true international icons. The first obvious choice is Terry Fox, the one-legged runner who inspired millions of Canadians before he eventually lost his fight with cancer in 1981. Back in 1981, I was thirteen. But even at thirteen, I remember being profoundly impressed by young Terry's courage.

To say that Terry Fox's legacy casts a fairly big shadow is an understatement of the greatest magnitude. As far as I'm concerned, Terry was Canada's first real hero—no one else warrants an honourable mention.

After Terry, the *second* most popular choice for "local hero makes good" is probably Rick Hansen. Wheelchair athlete Rick Hansen gained international recognition after finishing his "Man in Motion" around-the-globe marathon in 1987 —the same year that I graduated from high school. Though perhaps not a cultural icon in the same way Terry Fox was, Hansen's world tour did a lot to raise the profile of handicapped people everywhere. He deserves ample kudos for that alone.

I happened to see Rick Hansen a few years after his marathon—just bumped into him—in a parking lot at the University of British Columbia. I was on my way to a class, and he was on his way to somewhere else.

As soon as I saw him, I was instantly nervous. The nerves were to be expected, I suppose. Attempting to squash my nerves, I approached.

"You don't know me," I said, "but I know you—and I would be honoured to shake your hand."

Rick Hansen smiled politely, said hello, and stuck out his hand obligingly.

My voice had cracked a little. My palms were sweaty, too. I hoped this had escaped notice, but I doubted it. Yes, years after completing his famous spin around the world, Rick Hansen remained an intimidating hero.

Given all of Rick Hansen's positive press, there was, however, one catchphrase he popularized that I had difficulty wrapping my head around. I remember seeing Hansen on TV back in 1987 (in front of cameras, microphones, and the media) when he coined the phrase "physically challenged." It was a new politically correct term meant to replace the well-used descriptors "physically disabled" and "physically handicapped."

"Physically challenged" immediately struck me as an odd pairing of words—two words that weren't meant to fit together whatsoever. A weird juxtaposition. The epitome of an oxymoron. Jumbo shrimp. Deafening silence. Pretty ugly. Almost exactly. Definite maybe. Constant variable.

Physically challenged. I didn't like it, not at all. The term was far too vague, too open-ended. Anyone could be physically challenged. An out-of-shape couch potato could easily fit the bill, for instance. Or even Steve Nash, a world-class hoopster, would most likely feel "physically challenged" trying to play a game of wheelchair basketball.

Apologies to Mr. Hansen, but "physically challenged" was a downright confusing term. It pointed to nothing concrete and, in essence, reduced the significance of an actual physical disability to almost nothing. But a physical disability is a lot more than nothing. I mean, I know what Rick Hansen was trying to do. It was a noble attempt to put all the people in wheelchairs, all the people with crutches, on a level playing field with everyone else.

But still, it's simply dishonest to minimize the disability too much. Lifelong physical disabilities represent a serious hardship to those people who have them and, therefore, should be weighted accordingly.

Me, I've always liked the term "physically handicapped" best. The golfers have it right. A golf handicap, just like a physical one, freely acknowledges the need for an assist (a stroke or two) to even things out and make the competition fairer. And really, there's nothing wrong with that. At the end of the day, handicap or no, we all deserve a chance to play the same game.

My lifelong handicap represents a lot more than a physical challenge. Sometimes, it reminds me of all that is impossible. My lovely, wheelchair-confined wife and I, for example, can't walk hand-in-hand together. We can hold hands, sure, but not while walking. I can't enjoy a snuggle on the sofa with my wife, either. Elana can't sit on the sofa—any sofa. A simple thing for most people, but not for her.

It is all these simple, everyday things where a physical disability can really get you down. And that's when a term like "physically challenged" seems horribly inadequate.

Some days, having a physical disability can be rough. Deep rough. Sometimes, I am like a frustrated golfer—after landing a shot smack in the middle of a difficult sand trap. But like any good golfer, I take a moment to recompose myself, acknowledge my handicap and, for better or worse, play on...

"ALL RIGHT, SO MAYBE BEING DIFFERENT ISN'T SO BAD AFTER ALL!"

DIFFERENT: "Unlike in form, quality, amount, or nature; dissimilar. Distinct or separate."
(WWW.THEFREEDICTIONARY.COM)

Everyone out there has a handicap of some sort. But not all handicaps are readily visible. My elbow crutches and bent legs are fairly noticeable. Other handicaps, though, are a lot harder to spot.

Yet in truth, we all have flaws. We all face obstacles; everybody struggles with something. It is our struggles that ultimately shape who we are and determine the person we will become. When adversity strikes, some people crumble. Others discover inner strength and perseverance to rise above it.

My physical disability has shaped me, too, and mostly for the better. My struggles have given me added wisdom, patience, and empathy, and while it is true that I have always had a very healthy dose of self-confidence (some might even say a cocky confidence at times), my handicap has humbled me. I have always said (and only half-jokingly) that were it not for my disability, I would have grown up to be a somewhat pompous, mildly annoying jerk.

My disability alone does not define me, but it is nonetheless an important part of who I am. In my quest to fit in with the "normal" able-bodied crowd (particularly in my early Chaffey Burke days), I would sometimes try to push my physical handicap off to the side. Try to ignore it. Sweep my disability (and hide my crutches) under the figurative rug.

As I have alluded to before, the word "different" has always carried a negative connotation for me. I do much prefer focusing on similarities. Most of my life, it is true, was spent striving for acceptance, to fit in, to be like everyone else, to be normal. I do not think that I have ever tried to fully deny my handicap, but still, I *am* guilty of sometimes trying to distance myself from it. Especially when starting out at Chaffey Burke (my first real crack at an attempt to be "normal"), I made a very conscious effort to cut ties to any and all things "DISABLED." I immediately dumped all of my handicapped friends at G.F. Strong. For many years afterward, I would go out of my way to avoid all possible contact with other disabled folk. Yes, in my undying quest to be accepted as "normal," essentially, I did whatever I thought needed to be done.

Looking back on everything, I now know that trying to put deliberate distance between my disability and myself as a person was probably unnecessary. I know now that my disability is an integral part of who I am. My disability, my struggles, my victories… these have all shaped who I am as a person. To separate me from my disability is all but impossible. To ignore my handicap, or in any way minimize its importance in my life, would be equivalent to me throwing out, or completely disregarding, big chunks of my personality.

Trying to be too much like everybody else can hurt you. It's true. Being fully comfortable with your whole person—quirks, flaws, warts and all—is the only way to uncover your truest sense of self, embracing your differences, your struggles… your everything. That is your most genuine self.

And so now it appears that I have come full circle. To be seen as different (anything other than "normal") used to be something I liked to avoid. Now, I don't mind that label as much.

It's strange to reflect back and see how much I've changed regarding my whole preoccupation with "different versus normal." Gradually, very slowly, I have allowed myself to be transformed bit by bit. The further I crept into adulthood, it seems, the closer I came to a complete temporal shift in my brain.

But I suppose it really wasn't until I had reached my thirty-third year of life that my temporal shift—my newest revelation—fully cemented itself. See, it wasn't until I was over three-quarters into my thirty-third year that I fell in love... fell truly in love with a woman, for real. Once Elana came into my life, I discovered a whole different side of myself—as well as several other nooks and crannies that had remained unexplored.

With Elana in my life, I transformed even further.

MY PAST EXPERIENCES
WITH LOVE & GIRLFRIENDS
(VERSUS FRIENDLY GIRLS)

For all of my cocky confidence growing up, I have always been a rather awkward Casanova when it came to meeting girls (and women). In fact, I didn't experience my first serious relationship until just after graduating high school, when I was nineteen. Before then, the idea of love and of girlfriends really scared me.

Which isn't to say that I wasn't still a bit spooked at nineteen. I was. Looking back on everything, I can now freely admit that a big part of my awkwardness and fear came from me not being completely honest with myself, as well as not being more upfront about my disability.

See, I had convinced myself long ago (long before I ever started to become interested in girls) that I never wanted to date or marry, or even become casual friends with anyone who had a physical handicap. Again, my stubborn "I Just Wanna Be Normal" attitude was to blame here.

From the end of high school to the beginning of college, and all the way through my last years of university and beyond, I only considered dating able-bodied women. The mere thought of trying to date a woman with a physical disability—well, it just seemed like a lot of work. Dealing with my own handicap 24/7 was a big enough challenge, I thought. Having to somehow handle a whole other *second* disability? An even bigger burden, surely.

In any case, I stumbled on through a full fifteen years of life, and only really ever had two serious relationships during that entire span. I had little problem hooking up with any of the many girls who were into the whole strictly platonic thing. But of course, like any regular guy, I was hoping—eventually—that I'd end up with something a bit more substantial. I wasn't asking for much. I just wanted to find one girl—that one special woman—and that's it.

Despite my obvious struggles with dating, I remained firmly convinced that, ultimately, love and relationships with able-bodied women was somehow easier. And thinking back to my first serious girlfriend at age nineteen, well, yes, in truth that actually was pretty easy. At nineteen, life is simple—and so is love. All my girlfriend ever wanted of me was to hang out, have fun, and kiss each other lots at every opportunity. This was a pretty easy order to fill. At nineteen, love was scary at times, true, and yet, in the final analysis, it was also amazingly simple.

It's funny how the older you get, the more layered love becomes. And as if love wasn't already hard enough to figure out, throwing a pair of crutches and a physical disability into the mix added yet another wrinkle. Back when I was nineteen and in love, my crutches were honestly no big deal. As I moved into my early twenties, though, I discovered an interesting generalization about women. The older a woman gets, the choosier she becomes, especially when it comes to love, romance, and marriage. So while there were still plenty of women out there, I'm sure, willing to give me a fair shot, plenty of others were not. Because when the competition gets fierce, only the strong can survive. And let's face it, in the eyes of many, a guy with bent legs is a sure bet to be an early casualty.

To be fair, though, it isn't only the women at fault here. I accept at least fifty percent of the blame, maybe more. After all, I had difficulty getting past the bent legs and crutches *myself* sometimes! Yes, by refusing to let go of that "I Just Wanna Be Normal" mindset, I was setting myself up for inevitable disappointment and failure. Because whether I liked it or not, I *was* different. My handicap and crutches made me different. Yes, it may have been okay to strive for acceptance amongst able-bodied peers (and girlfriends), but regardless, my physical disability would always make me at least a little bit different. I could never exactly measure up with those lucky enough to be able-bodied. And more than anything else, it was all those niggly insecurities I had about my own disability (niggly things that I didn't really see). When stacked up against an able-bodied woman, well, truthfully, I never felt like a complete man. My disability, and especially my attempts to ignore it, prevented me from feeling like a complete, worthy package. I still had my confidence most of the time, sure, but when it came to my friendships with women and my attempts to move them forward into more serious, discriminating territory, well, I never really had a firm grasp of precisely where I stood. Whenever I felt the ground wobble beneath my feet, I would just bulldoze right on through.

Eventually, though, running through my head at some critical make-it-or-break-it moment, were really important questions like, *"Will I make a good boyfriend?"* or *"Will I make a good future husband, be a good provider, or be successful in marriage?"* Or finally, the ultimate question, *"Does my girlfriend think that I am* able *enough for her, or is my disability too much for her to handle?"* I hated that last question most of all. Rather than make a serious attempt to round-table that question, I would avoid it altogether. My disability became a white elephant. Big, unwieldy, and overstuffed.

By the time I had moved on to my second girlfriend, and what turned out to be my last attempt at a relationship before finally finding myself with Elana some ten years later, love had become a lot more complicated.

At twenty-three, and in my second year of university, I figured that I was finally mature enough—and better equipped—to handle love. This second girlfriend came a full four years after my first one. She was twenty-six. When we first met, she was just getting out of a bad relationship with an abusive boyfriend, and I suppose that should have been a big enough red flag for me right there. Looking back now, it is clear that I was her "Rebound Guy," her confidante. But love is blind, as they say.

Right when we first started dating, she made it very clear that she wanted to start off slow, take an easy pace, and not rush into another serious relationship (like her last one). It was very important to her that we start out as "Just Friends." For the most part, I was okay with that. I mean, I could tell that she really liked me. She would tell me all the time how important I was to her. She confided intimate secrets, her most private thoughts. An entire heart and soul laid bare for me. Unfortunately, though, all this baring of souls was more than I could handle. As time went on, I found myself having really strong feelings for her. Eventually, I couldn't help but fall in love with her. I only wish I had paid better attention to that big red flag, though, because I fell hard.

For one and a half years, I stayed patient, waiting for her to fall in love with me, too. But she never did. Despite all the hefty praise thrown my way, despite all her sharing of secrets—yes, in spite of everything, I never broke out of the "Just Friends" zone. For one and a half years, I struggled hard to keep my true feelings under wraps, wondering if they would ever be reciprocated. But her feelings towards me never really changed.

When the relationship finally ended, the break-up hit me hard. For weeks afterward, I studied every busted part, piece by piece. In the end, I conceded that love was a puzzle. And no matter how hard I tried, some pieces just weren't meant to fit where I expected them to.

An entire decade passed before I would come across love again. At thirty-three, the long wait would finally be over. In December 2001, Elana made her grand entrance, and for the first time ever, love's intricate puzzle pieced together exactly as it should.

MOVING TOWARDS
MARRIAGE AND A LIFE
WITH ELANA

Meeting Elana immediately challenged my long-held opinions about love, and about how relationships with women were supposed to work. My marriage and life with Elana has forever changed me. With Elana, I could finally embrace my physical disability without hesitation. I could finally reveal the truest version of myself without fear.

I first met Elana on a blind date, on December 1, 2001. Though, to be honest, I didn't go into that first date *completely* "blind." The older sister of a lifelong friend of mine was my matchmaker. This sister/matchmaker had just met Elana herself, a week or so previous. She and Elana just happened to cross paths one afternoon, a brief impromptu meeting. It was just long enough, apparently, to strike up a friendly conversation—and, yes, just long enough for Elana to make a favourable first impression. From there, events unfolded in such a way that a launch from cupid's arrow was utterly unavoidable.

My friend's sister (a.k.a. the matchmaker) phoned me later that same day. Since she never was one to call me out of the blue like that, right away I knew something was up.

"I just met the perfect woman for you," she says to me. "She's perfect. You and her share a lot of things in common, and she has a personality very similar to yours, too. She's the female equivalent of you…"

The sister/matchmaker rambled on: Elana was twenty-five (with a birthday coming up fast on December 8), an elementary school teacher, a singer, had a physical disability, and used a motorized wheelchair to get around.

Of course, I was a bit put off at the mention of her physical disability. Undaunted, though, the sister proceeded to go on and on about how beautiful Elana was. Knowing my matchmaker as someone not prone to exaggeration, I have to say that I was baited pretty quick.

And so, that very same night, and despite some initial hesitation, I picked up the phone and made my first call to Elana. Our initial conversation lasted for almost two hours! I don't remember what we talked about, but I do remember being pleasantly surprised at how easy and natural the whole exchange was. Elana had left me with a very good first impression, no question. I got an immediate sense of her tremendous energy and fierce independence, tightly woven together with an equal measure of gentleness, politeness, and warmth. All that, and a truly sexy telephone-voice to boot. Still, I knew that the real test of potential compatibility and chemistry would have to wait until our first actual face-to-face encounter.

A few days later, then, after a couple more phone calls and swapped photos via e-mail, I suggested a fairly casual first meeting at the neighbourhood mall. I figured getting an early start on Christmas shopping might make for a fun first date. So it was that the afternoon of December 1 was set as our official unveiling to each other.

I was still a bit nervous about the whole "blind date" thing, though. I mean, yes, my phone conversations with

Elana had all gone pretty well, but regardless, I really didn't know what to expect of her in person. For one thing, the photo that she had e-mailed to me a few days previous was essentially the size of a postage stamp. Not only was the detail of the photo a bit fuzzy, but she was wearing dark sunglasses in the picture as well! So I had no real idea what Elana looked like. I was going into this first date quite blind, indeed. I just had to trust my instincts.

Still, doubts started creeping into my head. I thought to myself, *Suppose this Elana girl is beautiful, as sister/matchmaker said? Do I want a woman in a wheelchair? Isn't my own physical disability enough to handle already?*

But then I realized how hypocritical I was being. After all, wasn't I sometimes complaining that women weren't giving me a fair shot because they were scared off by my disability? Didn't Elana deserve a fair shot, too? Tossing those questions around for a while, I decided that I was going to give this first date an honest chance to succeed.

As the afternoon of my blind date with Elana approached, I knew that it was important for me to stay relaxed, to not feel rushed. I wanted to make a good first impression, obviously. So I took an extra early bus up to the mall to guarantee I'd be there on time.

Little did I know that Elana preferred to err on the side of fashionably late. And so, here I was, hanging out in the food court, the designated rendezvous spot, waiting. And waiting. And waiting some more.

I waited for almost forty minutes, I think. Keeping an eye out for a woman in a motorized wheelchair should have been an easy task. Except on this day, a Saturday afternoon, motorized wheelchairs of every make and model, it seemed, were out in full force. It was like a wheelchair parade. In the space of about forty minutes, I must have seen at least a full dozen motorized chairs.

But, then, just as my eyeballs were getting dizzy from all of that tracking, Elana suddenly appeared from around the corner and I knew instantly that she was finally the one—the one I'd been waiting for.

I wasn't focused on her wheelchair at all, though. Right from the first moment, I didn't see it. The only thing I remember thinking, repeatedly, was: *Wow, this girl is beautiful. Cute, sexy, beautiful... everything.* And from that moment, Elana's wheelchair just melted away from underneath her.

It was actually much later, after dating Elana for a few months, that I learned to see the side-benefit of being with a disabled girlfriend, the perk being that *she knew* that I knew (that she knew that *I knew*) that having to deal with a physical disability on a daily basis was difficult. We both pretty much shared the same measuring stick—no unfair comparisons to able bodies, no white elephant.

I approached my courtship with Elana with total confidence, far outstripping anything I had experienced before. I was more sure-footed, the ground no longer feeling shaky beneath me. I didn't have to hide my disability or push it off to the side. With Elana, I could be the full, genuine me.

In my marriage and life with Elana, I finally feel like a complete man. Yes, I even feel like the strong hero sometimes, performing a daring rescue.

Except, really, it was Elana that rescued me. An early Christmas gift from the heavens, Elana was God's answer to my selfish prayer. In my non-Christian days, I didn't pray very much, it's true. But after enduring several months of consecutive first-date disappointments back-to-back-to-back, and with my frustration at an all-time high and my confidence bruised and battered beyond recognition, I actually did one day end up praying for God to send a woman who would truly love me, crutches and all. It was undoubtedly the most selfish, honest prayer I had ever prayed in my whole life up to that point. And to my amazement, God listened. He heard every selfish word of that prayer—and ultimately delivered far, far more than I ever thought possible.

God knew what I wanted, yes. But even more importantly, God saw what I actually needed, too. Seeing that I was ready to reach for Him, God offered up two special people—Elana, the woman of my dreams, and Jesus, my saviour. Of course, at first blush, this Express Post package from the Almighty was something I had not expected—on both counts. But there again, it was without question something extremely precious and priceless, something that I needed, a thing I had been lacking for thirty-three years. It was a gift most gracious— literally. A small, but very important thing...

It was the gift of salvation, and an amazing love. What's even more surprising to me is how something that I needed became exactly everything that I ever wanted, and then some.

I HEART ELANA

"Love is patient, love is kind."
(1 CORINTHIANS 13:4)

Most everybody seems to agree that, between Elana and myself, I am the more patient person. Take a quick anonymous poll of all our friends and family—both Elana's and mine combined—and I would probably come out on top every time.

But that assessment is neither fair, nor accurate. The truth is, Elana has one of the most patient, open, honest, accepting, and trusting hearts there is. I mean, when Elana and I first hooked up together, quite a few of her Christian friends voiced their disapproval; said that she shouldn't even entertain the idea of a non-Christian boyfriend. But, you see, Elana was able to unveil the potential in me right away. She was willing to give me the benefit of the doubt and to show patience.

A lot of Christians have trouble being inclusive or open to different points of view. Rather than show patience, many Christians prefer the safer route: preaching to the choir, so to speak, to the already converted. I see Elana operating outside of her safe zone a lot though, in her faith, in her career as a school teacher, and in demonstrating the love she has for me. Elana amazes me and inspires me. I may have fallen in love with her drive, determination, intelligence, wit, beauty, and sexiness, but, without question, it is Elana's patient heart for which I am eternally thankful.

THE MARRIAGE
PROPOSAL

In the early days of our courtship, I remember telling Elana how our first date felt like a tenth date, how the second felt like a twentieth... and the third one, like a thirtieth. I also told her that in my past relationships with women I had always been a bit of a slow-mover, always extra-cautious. And to this day, Elana still doesn't believe me. Though I can't say that I blame her, really.

With Elana, I broke with tradition in a big, big way. I became more relaxed, assured, and confident the more time I spent with her. Instead of having to squash feelings of inadequacy, as I had in the past with able-bodied girlfriends, I was suddenly a lot braver—a lot more sure of what I wanted.

Valentine's Day, 2002: Two and a half months after our first blind date, I felt the pressure to be romantic. Of course. And so that was the day I told Elana, for the very first time, that I was falling in love with her. And I really was. Truthfully, I already knew that I wanted to marry her. I didn't dare tell Elana that, though—no, I didn't want to freak her out quite yet.

I always told Elana that we needed to put a reasonable chunk of time into the "Boyfriend-Girlfriend Courtship" phase—a good year, at least—before moving on to our next phases of engagement, and then marriage.

That was my plan, anyway. But I went ahead of schedule and bought Elana's engagement ring a full two months early. Not only was I sure to surprise Elana, but I surprised myself, too. I mean, I didn't even have a job at that particular time, either—not the best time to be buying a ring. I couldn't help myself, though—it just felt right.

September 27, 2002: The day I would ask Elana to marry me. I struggled with ideas for how exactly I was going to propose to her. Again, I wanted it to be romantic. I thought of popping the question at a nice restaurant, maybe—but even then, I worried that there would be too many distractions. I needed something simple, and straightforward, a quiet place with just me, Elana, and nothing else. Eventually, I settled on the plan of taking Elana for a long walk—simple, straightforward… and maybe even a touch romantic (or so I hoped).

When Elana came over to my house later that afternoon, I was ready and waiting for her. She had barely gotten her wheelchair down off the lowered ramp of the HandyDart bus when I launched into action.

"Want to go for a walk?"

Right away, Elana could tell I was behaving a bit odd. She could sense that I felt hurried, but she didn't yet know why. In any event, Elana nevertheless agreed to my casual, spontaneous request.

A few moments later and we were walking together down a long paved path near my house. Elana and I had strolled down this path a few times before and, only a few steps into our walk, I suddenly remembered why Elana didn't particularly like this path—it was too narrow. Yes, the entirety of the path was paved with nice smooth asphalt, but the strip of pavement was a bit on the thin side. Not usually a big problem, except the grass on either side of it was typically soft and boggy—a bit treacherous for a heavy motorized wheelchair.

Since it was too much of a tight squeeze to walk side-by-side, I was forced to trail a little behind the wheelchair. Right away, Elana was irritated, though. Whenever we took walks together, Elana preferred to be right alongside me. Any walk where we couldn't be side-by-side wasn't worth taking, in her opinion. So my little romantic plan was off to a rough start. Unbeknownst to me, it was about to get rougher still. For the record, though, I just want to say that it was all Elana's fault—she was trying to squeeze in, side-by-side...

I remember thinking, *This is the moment—right here, right now!* I was ready to pop the question. I was just about to reach into my pocket for the engagement ring, when—at that precise moment—it happened. Elana's wheelchair began to lean to one side; very slowly tip. Still focused on the ring concealed in my pocket, though (and on what I was about to do), I almost didn't notice it. By the time I did notice, it was already too late. I reached an arm out, but it didn't help.

The wheelchair crashed to the ground, with Elana tumbling out and rolling clear. Those first few seconds were mild horror, at minimum. But after that first initial shock wore off, I realized Elana was still perfectly intact. All things considered, the fall had been a relatively gentle one. There she was, laying on the grass, staring up into the sun, squinting. Elana was a bit dazed, yes, but after breathing my requisite sigh of relief, I stood there looking down at her, marvelling at just how lovely she looked to me right then.

A couple of strong men passing by got Elana upright and back in her wheelchair, and after the commotion had subsided, I plunged ahead with my task of asking Elana to marry me.

"So, do you know what day it is today?" I ask.

"What?"

"Do you know what day it is today?" I asked again.

"I, uh... no. Is it somebody's birthday?"

"You really don't know what day it is?"

Elana pauses, thinks hard. I can see confusion creeping in.

"No. No, I don't," she says.

I reach into my pocket and pull out the ring.

"Today is the day that I'm going to ask you to marry me!"

Elana was still suffering the aftereffects of her little tumble… still dazed.

"What? I don't get—? But how did—? Are you *sure?*"

Not exactly the response I was expecting. So I wait for maybe two or three additional seconds, hoping Elana might say something a bit more coherent, more intelligible.

"Really? But I don't get it… I thought you wanted to wait," she says.

Okay, this was somewhat better. Elana was speaking in full sentences now.

Even so—not quite the answer I was looking for. I pressed on, undaunted.

"So, is that a yes, then?"

"Oh. Oh yeah. Yes. Yes, of course!" says Elana with her big beaming smile.

Whew. Finally. A *yes!* Just like that, I was suddenly officially engaged. Very cool. No, the whole marriage proposal didn't exactly go as I had planned—but hey, it had all worked out!

It's a pretty crazy proposal story, though. And, of course, during those first few months of being engaged, of being a new fiancé, there were a lot of friends and family that wanted to hear all about it. I loved retelling everything: our romantic walk down a tad-too-narrow asphalt path, the wheelchair tipping over, and Elana tumbling out. The final punchline was always the best part: *"And that's when Elana fell head-over-heels for me…"*

Looking back, I realize how Elana's fall added a little extra pizzazz to everything. God had a hand in it, I know. He had been there from the very beginning, and it's further proof that our Almighty Creator has a wonderful sense of comedic timing.

DISABILITY +
DISCRIMINATION = BAD

DISCRIMINATION: "Unfair treatment of a person, racial group, or minority."
(WWW.THEFREEDICTIONARY.COM)

My whole life, I have experienced extreme prejudice towards my disability only once. Just one particular time in my life, and that's it. I suppose I should count my blessings—but now, over fifteen years later, it still bothers me that my one bad experience with discrimination had to happen at all.

Obviously, there is no good time or place for prejudice. Discrimination sucks, plain and simple—no matter when it strikes. For me, it happened at university, in my second year of training to become an elementary school teacher. More specifically, it happened during my final practicum as a student teacher.

For this final three-month practicum, I had been placed in a Grade Five class. The classroom teacher that I was to work with, and learn from, Ms. Alden, had over thirty years of on-the-job experience. You'd think that thirty years of know-how would have been a tremendous boon to me (as the inexperienced student teacher I was), but alas, no. Unfortunately for me, Ms. Alden was a little too set in her "old school" ways—and everything she preached stood in direct opposition to what I was learning at university. Small groups, cooperative learning, and creative activities were at the forefront of my teaching strategies... but yet, all of these things were completely foreign to Ms. Alden.

As if Ms. Alden's "old school" tendencies weren't enough for me to contend with, it got worse. Not only did I have to impress my classroom teacher, Ms. Alden, but I also got paired up with an equally-challenged "old school" university administrator. The university administrator was someone who was *supposed* to be there for me—a key support, a cheerleader, an encourager. And yet it never really worked out that way—we were always butting heads, it seems.

With Ms. Alden and my faculty administrator joining forces from the get-go, I never honestly stood a chance of success. It didn't matter that I had aced all of my earlier practicum experiences and course material—no, I was doomed to fail from Day One.

For starters, my faculty advisor, with a background in Special Education, was always telling me to dumb-down my lesson plans. Always. It didn't matter what I did, my lesson plans were never quite dumb enough. Given his strong personal bias, any lesson or activity which encouraged too much creative energy from my Grade Five students was deemed "high-level": in other words, too much of a challenge and, therefore, inappropriate.

I remember one lesson in particular. I had all of my students conjure up their own time-machine designs, as an alternative to the magical wardrobe in *The Chronicles of Narnia*. I asked the students to draw, color, and label all the important parts of their individual creations, and then, finally, to write a short paragraph to advertise and explain how the whole machine works. I was incredibly pleased with the creativity and the tremendous variety put on display. The result: thirty students, with thirty completely different and unique designs. But while I was impressed, my faculty advisor was not. His criticism: too creative... too open-ended... not enough structure. My advisor suggested that I should have used a poster from the time-travel movie *Back to the Future*—this would have given the students more creative guidance and structure, he argued. To prove his point, he somehow managed to track down a small picture of the classic *Back to the Future* poster, then asked five students to draw *another* time-machine... only this time, to use the shiny silver Delorean as inspiration.

Needless to say, I wasn't the least bit surprised when all five students copied the design of the Delorean *exactly*... right down to the last bolt! And yet, in spite of these boring, highly predictable results, my advisor for some strange reason remained thoroughly convinced that his little exercise had yielded much better results. Not satisfied to stop there, I watched my advisor dig through his briefcase. A few moments later, he pulled out a few sheets of paper. The papers were mostly blank, but had the same thing drawn in the center of each page—a picture of a large power switch, with a bolded "ON" at the top end of its handle, and an "OFF" at the bottom. Again, he took the same five students and asked them to draw a *third* version of their time machines... using the sheet provided. Right away, I told him that all five students were going to draw a large rectangular box around the main on-off switch, and adorn it with a few additional computerized buttons and switches. At the end of this third exercise/demonstration, my prediction was 100% correct. Except, again, it didn't seem to matter. The faculty advisor was pleased-as-punch at the results. To this day, I still don't understand it.

Of course, I could go on with many more examples. With each passing day—with my collection of little failures growing larger and larger—I could see my entire practicum, and my whole career as a school teacher, slowly unravel. My dream of becoming a teacher was a big goal—something that I spent the last five years of my life working extremely hard for. And to see it wither and die before my own eyes in amazing Technicolor was extremely discouraging, disheartening, and painful.

It is quite clear to me now how both the classroom teacher and my faculty advisor set me up for a fall. They assumed I would fail, and so, like a self-fulfilling prophecy, I did. As if I didn't already know that my own crutches and disability were obstacles enough, they both threw even more barriers at me. They both assumed, right off the bat I'm sure, that my physical disability was going to be too much for me. And really, though they each could have chosen to make things a little easier for me, or help me to adapt different teaching strategies, they both made that all-important decision to make everything just a wee bit harder. When I struggled a little with writing things up on the blackboard (my chalk writing can be a bit messy), they both said that if I couldn't write properly then I shouldn't be teaching. Early on, I had wanted to enlist the help of my students to write things for me, but I was told no, absolutely not—it couldn't be done. They also said that I had bad posture in front of the class. Sorry, but I can't straighten my bent legs! I wanted to hold weekly classroom meetings, too, in an effort to improve morale and student behaviour. *Classroom meetings don't work and are a waste of valuable learning time,* I was told. Every week, I would bring up my idea of holding a class meeting, and every week Ms. Alden said no.

Things progressed from bad to worse—a lot worse. I even got yelled at and sternly reprimanded (for a full twenty minutes, at least) when I arrived a few minutes late one very cold winter morning due to car trouble. The kicker was that I don't even drive. It wasn't my car. I was carpooling to school with the other student-teacher. It was her car, she was driving, and yet she received no similar reprimand from the exact same faculty advisor—nothing at all. According to her, there wasn't the slightest mention of it.

In the end, about three weeks short of completing my final practicum, I was forced to quit—and was ultimately booted from the Education program. To hear them tell it, I was a good teacher, good with the students, and truly a real inspiration. Here it was, the end of the road for me, and they kept showering me with compliments. It was too little too late, and I didn't understand why they would go to such lengths to start throwing praises at me now. I mean, honestly, why bother? If I was such a great teacher, as they said (repeatedly), then why was I being asked to leave? It's just not going to work out, they said. Again, it didn't make any sense to me at all. I tried to launch a formal complaint with the Dean of Education, but it didn't help.

As I have already alluded to, it was a pretty clear case of disability discrimination. Two prejudiced people sealed my fate. Too bad for me, but I guess I had tried to blaze a trail a few years too early. For some, me and my crutches, and my dream of becoming a teacher, was asking too much, too soon.

Ms. Alden asked me to come back for one last visit with the students two weeks after my practicum was terminated. I didn't really feel like doing it, but she was persistent and eventually I relented. The students were happy to see me. They told me how much they had missed me. That was nice to hear, I guess. But then Ms. Alden told me how she had decided to adopt my idea of weekly classroom meetings, and said that I was right about how they could help with student morale and behaviour. Ms. Alden proudly stated that she had held two classroom meetings thus far, and both had worked wonderfully! Somehow, she must have honestly thought that I would appreciate the compliment, but it was a bitter blow, a cruel knife to the heart—and I was suddenly wishing that I hadn't bothered to show up at the school for a visit in the first place.

To see my wife Elana achieve her success as a school teacher (only two years after my attempt) was further proof that I had indeed been shortchanged. But even so, that doesn't stop me from being extremely proud of what Elana was able to accomplish. She had triumphed where I had failed. My wife's disability is much worse than mine; her obstacles far greater. It really is astonishing to me how a couple of years—and one or two more supportive, helpful people—made all the difference to her success. Whereas my blackboard scribble was inexcusable, the fact that Elana can't write on a black-board at all no longer matters. And while my bad posture and bent legs were seen as a very serious problem, my wife in her wheelchair has been sitting pretty as a successful, inspirational teacher for over a dozen years now.

MOVING ON TO
ANOTHER DREAM

With my teaching career over before it even started, I had to move on to something else. Right away, I made the decision to finish the fourth year of my Bachelor of Arts degree—and worry about settling on another career choice later.

Overall, my experience at university was a very good one. Yes, I had that one bad failed practicum, but to me, education is never wasted. I still had a blast—I loved learning new things and making new friends. I liked everything about my four years on campus, and I wouldn't change any of it.

Upon completing my B.A., my tough choices of embarking on a career and a real life began. Through a job-finding agency, I landed on my feet working full-time for the provincial government as a Public Servant. I already had a natural knack for computers and I was soon put to work organizing digital records and building small-scale databases. After only a month or two on the job, it was obvious to me that a long career in computers was to be my new dream.

In 1998, I decided to get even more serious about a career in computers—and after mastering over six months' worth of ridiculously difficult and in-depth course material, I was finally (and officially) a Microsoft Certified Systems Engineer (MCSE).

Since earning my MCSE designation, I have continued to find relatively steady employment in the IT industry. I have now spent a good dozen years either tinkering with databases, working as a technical support analyst, or engaging in some other form of customer service.

Life threw me a bit of a curveball when my teaching practicum imploded on me, but somehow everything turned out pretty well. Sometimes, even the best laid plans don't come to fruition—and usually, it's because God has something even better in store.

Over the years, I've learned to trust God more. I have learned to take life easier, and to take better care of myself health-wise. I have never smoked cigarettes and I rarely drink—maybe the odd festive rum and eggnog, but that's pretty much it. I also get regular chiropractic adjustments every five weeks. Growing up with a physical disability, I learned early to respect my body. The older my body gets, the more I'm learning to respect it. It really frustrates me to see teenagers nowadays, those with perfectly functioning bodies (fully working legs, lungs, and everything else) purposely harming themselves, sabotaging their health with bad habits: cigarettes, drugs, and alcohol. Essentially, it's like *voluntarily* taking on a physical disability. It's sad to see so many people self-medicating through dangerous addictions, especially considering how God has blessed the vast majority with health and an able body right from the start. Even before I became a Christian, I always knew my body was a temple. To disrespect your body—to harm it in any way—is to dishonour God. I firmly believe that.

So I try my best to look after myself. I'm not perfect, no, but I do try. And while I've never been accused of being a Type A personality, by any stretch of the imagination, I'm quite careful not to overexert myself now that I'm older. I no longer live to work. I only work to live, and honestly, I'd be quite happy to retire to a more laid-back, lazy life. That way, I'd have more time to spend with my wife and son, as well as more time to work on my photography and my writing.

OUR SON,
JAKE TORY

Growing up, I always assumed that I'd be married by age twenty-five and have kids by thirty. As it turned out, I was married at thirty-five and a new father at forty. Funny how life unfolds in a way you don't expect.

I always wanted to be married with a kid or two someday, though. I assumed that it would happen, like some inevitable event. But sometimes, things don't materialize exactly when you expect them to. For me, that all-important realization hit right about the time I turned thirty. Turning thirty is a bit of a watershed birthday for most people, I think—and it's a time to pause, reflect, and take stock of your life thus far. Well, it was for me anyway.

So here I was at thirty, with no girlfriend, no wife, no marriage, and no children. I was thirty years of age and not at all where I had expected to be. But I didn't really want to feel sorry for myself. Instead, I simply started revising my expectations for whatever lay ahead of me: my future. I just started thinking that maybe, possibly, I wouldn't ever get married, wouldn't ever have children and become a father. And slowly, I began to be sort of okay with all of that.

When I think back on my life before Elana, before my six years of marriage, and before Jake—well, I really can't help but give my head a very hard shake! I almost can't remember myself at thirty anymore—that person is a complete stranger to me now.

●●◆●●

Elana and I started talking seriously about having kids maybe four years ago, or thereabouts. But to be perfectly honest, Elana was a lot more gung-ho towards the idea of having children than I was—in the beginning, at least. In our early discussions, I had difficulty wrapping my brain around the whole concept of starting a family, I admit. Again, as I have already said, after waiting so long to have kids, and after revising my expectations back at age thirty... well, truly, I had kind of gotten used to the notion of not having kids, that it wasn't supposed to happen. Over time, though, I began to warm up to it again. Eventually, a switch flipped off in my head and, just like that, I was once and for all firmly committed to becoming a dad. I really wanted it.

After that, we started planning for a family in earnest. I still had some concerns, though, some reservations. For one, ever since I can remember, I always wondered how effective or useful I would be as a father. Given my disability, I always envisioned that the first few years of parenthood would be especially tough for me. That strong belief had long been with me—even if I had somehow ended up with an able-bodied woman, instead of Elana, I still would have carried the exact same fear (or concern or worry). That was a big thing to work through.

As much as I was excited about our family planning and the prospect of being a father, these feelings were often tempered by my mild trepidation and expectation of what our first few years of parenthood would be like. Aside from all of that—as if that wasn't enough to deal with already—my other big concern was for Elana herself. Of course, Elana's own physical disability was a whole other wrinkle. Being that my wife's body and mobility is severely limited, in a few ways at least, I needed to be absolutely convinced that she would be physically capable of carrying a baby to full-term, and with zero impact on her health and well-being. If I couldn't be guaranteed of at least that much, then, for me, having a baby would no longer be an option. Elana was far more important to me than any baby I could dream up or hope for. If having a baby put her anywhere near harm's way, then no, it wasn't worth the risk.

So before any absolute and final decision to have a baby was set in motion, I needed to be convinced that everything would be okay with her. We saw one doctor, then another. Both were unanimous that yes, Elana's body could withstand the rigors of pregnancy, a nine-month term and child birth (or Caesarean section) perfectly fine.

With that problem in check my mind turned to baby-making. Still, it didn't happen right away—the pregnancy, I mean. For us, it was two years of honest-to-goodness trying before getting that positive result.

I always told Elana that I wouldn't be fully and truly excited about the prospect of having a baby until it became more real, more tangible. When it actually happened, I'd be pumped and ready. But until then, well, I just couldn't get myself excited about something that wasn't here yet. That mindset is true of most guys, I think. Two years into the whole process of trying to make a baby, though, and I don't think Elana ever really believed me, that I could suddenly switch over into "Daddy Mode" when the time came.

But then it happened. In January 2008 (Elana will remember the exact day and time, of course), my wife peed on the stick, it turned the right color, and the screams of jubilation ensued. I had been taking a nap on our sofa when I heard the screams. I woke up to see Elana directly in front of me.

"I'm pregnant!" she says.

I almost didn't hear it. Those two words were barely audible; her voice almost a whisper, a hushed excitement, the shock and awe of the moment not fully felt yet. It was still slowly seeping in.

In a matter of seconds, I had already played back that moment, and those two words, three or four times over in my head. It was here, it was a reality, and I was ready. Waves of immense joy washed over me—I mean, wow! It was amazing. I was going to be a father. Nine months from now, I would be a dad. Elana saw my face, saw my excitement, and saw something in me change in an instant. Yes, my wife has been eating crow ever since.

●●◈●●

Elana and I told both our families about the pregnancy at around the fourteenth week. There were shocked faces all around, a lot of dropped jaws, and for me personally, this baby news exposed something in my parents that I did not expect. From the first moment we announced the pregnancy, my mom was genuinely excited for us, sure, but there was also an obvious sense of worry right away, too. Yes, Elana's parents must have had a few concerns of their own (regarding the overall safety of the pregnancy) but if so, they kept it to themselves. Ultimately, Elana's parents respected the fact that a couple's decision—our decision—to have children was an extremely intimate and personal one. They trusted that Elana and I knew what we were getting ourselves into.

With my parents, though, it was different. My mom, especially. Yes, I can understand a mother's natural instinct to cushion her child from hurt, harm, and other difficult life experiences. I get that, I do. But from my perspective, my mom was a little too protective in this instance, a little too overbearing about the whole pregnancy thing. In my form-ative years, my mom had been instrumental in me learning to become self-sufficient, successful, and able, in spite of my physical handicap. Growing up, it was my mom and dad who instilled in me at a very early age the belief that I could accomplish anything, do anything. If I pushed on, tried really hard, there were no limits. Honestly, full credit goes to my parents for giving me a boundless confidence.

Considering all my parents taught me—and having been thoroughly convinced that I was capable of anything I set my mind to—I didn't completely understand my mom's level of concern. It struck me as strange, truly weird. After all, Elana and I had done our homework. We had not entered into this decision blind and unprepared. We thought hard about each and every possible obstacle, fully aware of the unique chal-lenges we would face as disabled parents.

Being disabled, Elana and I have both acquired a separate, very unique kind of wisdom—a wisdom born out of having lived and experienced our entire lives in broken bodies. As parents, my mom and dad may have a good second-hand knowledge and understanding of what it is like to be disabled, but they could never hope to give an accurate *firsthand* account of anything. Not without living it, as I have.

●●◆●●

Almost as soon as she found out she was pregnant, Elana started researching a bunch of stuff on the internet; anything to do with Baby's first year, or breast-feeding or whatever. She also made phone calls and wrote e-mails to track down people who could help make important modifications to her wheelchair, and come up with custom designs for all-new devices. Anything that would make it easier for Elana to be a better Mommy. Very soon we had a crib with a hinged door, and an altered hospital table to assist with breast-feeding. For transporting Baby, Elana and I settled on a very expensive "boutique" stroller. For holding Baby, Elana could wear a sling or—better yet—a particularly fancy custom-built baby seat that fastened via metal post to the front of her wheelchair. Despite her limited mobility, Elana was absolutely determined that she was going to be a "hands-on" Mom from the very beginning. As much as she *could* do without the help (or hands) of others, she would do.

In the process of trying to locate different people and resources, Elana couldn't find any other disabled couples like us where *BOTH* parents had a physical disability. In the entire province—the whole of British Columbia—Elana and I are quite possibly (…very probably) the only true pairing of two disabled parents. Who could have guessed that Elana and I would be parenting pioneers!

●●◆●●

Elana's whole pregnancy went amazingly well. Except for one little unexpected bump around the seventh week. Elana was at school, on her break in the photocopy room, when it happened. She felt something pop; felt something wet. Then she saw the blood; a fair bit, apparently. She left school as soon as possible and started rushing towards the hospital.

An ultrasound showed a heartbeat. Our very small baby, only about a half inch in size at that point, was fine. God was good. Elana was relieved, grateful. But then, later that same day, in the evening, it happened again. This time, Elana was at home with me, so I was there with her and saw everything. It was a lot of blood; by all accounts, much worse than the first episode that morning. By the time the ambulance came, Elana had bled out two large clots the size of baseballs.

The ambulance staff immediately assumed the worst, assumed the baby was lost. A spontaneous abortion, they called it. Very common in first pregnancies, they said. When we got to the hospital, they wheeled my wife in on a gurney and parked us in a small, tight hallway—just outside the emergency triage station. And there we sat, for several hours. Waiting. Wondering. Worrying. Praying. It was then, in those most desperate hours, that God revealed Himself in a most unexpected and amazing way. An elderly woman was parked in a gurney beside us, her husband there too, standing at the head of her bed, holding her hand, comforting her. The woman was in surprisingly good spirits, despite having taken a very bad fall only a couple of hours earlier (as I would soon find out). They were clearly a happy couple, and it really struck me— really made me stop and take notice. I mean, here they were, stuck in a cramped hallway of the hospital, and in their moment of personal crisis, they were still able to be completely jovial: smiling, talking, and laughing. I felt like a bit of a voyeur watching them, but I couldn't help it. Yes, this was somebody else's private moment, their moment, but it was also something that really impressed and moved me.

A few moments later, the elderly man and wife introduced themselves to us. With nothing else to do but wait, we talked. It was then that the husband shared the story of his wife's bad fall in detail.

Turning to face Elana, the woman asked, "So, why are you here, dear?"

My wife explained that she was seven weeks pregnant, how there had been a lot of blood, and how the ambulance staff had suspected it to be a spontaneous abortion.

The woman flashed a warm, knowing smile. "Don't worry," she said. "It will all work out just fine." Her words were spoken with such sincerity and gentleness. And for the first time, I felt comfort.

Then one of the elderly woman's daughters came to visit. And again, because there was nothing else to do but wait, the daughter soon struck up a conversation with us as well. Elana again talked about the pregnancy, the blood, and the spontaneous abortion.

"One of my daughters had a lot blood early on in her pregnancy, too," the woman's daughter said. "But her baby made it, totally healthy. Perfectly okay now."

Then the daughter offered to pray for us. I truly felt the presence of God, I mean, *really* felt Him. I was overwhelmed by a strange calmness and warmth. I heard God's voice, too. *Just wait*, He said. *Be reassured, and just wait.*

Elana finally got wheeled out of that cramped hallway and moved though the doors to the actual emergency triage. The attending doctor there tried to give Elana an ultrasound, but he couldn't get the machine to cooperate fully, for some reason. Looking up into the small computer monitor, I could see something fuzzy, but nothing distinct. There was no clear heartbeat.

Just wait. Be reassured, and just wait.

The doctor told us, again, to expect the worst, that a spontaneous abortion was likely inevitable. But I knew different. God was here. God was good, and He had promised us something very special; a miracle baby. All we had to do was wait.

●●◆●●

A few days later, I went with Elana for another ultrasound. This time, I could see the heartbeat quite clearly, the quick rhythmic pulses: *ba-ba, ba-ba, ba-ba…*

Our baby's tiny heart was still beating strong. Elana had bled out a lot, but our baby held on, was still clinging tight to the uterus wall like an acrobatic micro-sized superhero. We didn't even know the sex of the baby yet, but from that point on, Elana started to affectionately refer to him as Spiderman (or "Spidey," for short). Right then, I should have known—should have guessed—that we were going to have a baby boy.

●●◆●●

Baby Jake Tory was born on September 10, 2008 at 11:44 a.m.—delivered by Caesarean section. To finally see him, hold him for real—it was an incredible moment. I was in awe. Jake was perfect. God had delivered our miracle baby, as promised.

Some people have a tendency sometimes to overuse the word *miracle*. Like thinking, for instance, that our baby is a miracle simply because he was born to a disabled mom. These are often the same people who say that a disabled person is an inspiration by default, simply by having a disability.

People who toss around the word *miracle* so freely definitely irk Elana. And me, too. Yet there's no denying that our Jake is a miracle. No denying.

THE BIRTH ANNOUNCEMENT, VIA E-MAIL

September 10, 2008: The day of Jake's first scheduled appearance into this world was a busy one. Below is a largely-intact transcription of the original birth announcement that I typed up and sent off via e-mail early the next morning.

To all friends and family:

I am very proud to announce the arrival of a brand new baby Matheson.

My wife and I are the happy and awed parents of little boy Jake Tory—6 pounds, 10 ounces. Very healthy, and very cute. He was born at 11:44 a.m. and sent up to me by 12:30. Everything went well with Elana's C-Section, although she didn't get released from her "Recovery Room" until a little after 4:30 in the afternoon... which means she had to wait a full four hours longer than me before she saw the baby for the first time.

Our day started at 4:30 a.m., with arrival to hospital by 6:00. The C-Section surgery was scheduled to begin by around 7:30, but got delayed until about 11:30. After a long and eventful day, I didn't get home until around 9:00 p.m. for some much needed rest!

However, the plan is for me to stay at hospital as much as possible— including overnights—to learn as much as I can from the nursing staff about diaper changes, bathing, etc. I want to be prepared when we take Jake home. Elana's hospital stay will range anywhere from another four to nine days. Right now, the nurses are thinking it'll be six.

Both baby and mom are doing well. Elana called at 11:30 last night to say that little Jake had his first successful feeding. And Elana phoned again this morning to report that he has had even more success at the breast since. This little guy learns fast! Apparently, Jake spent much of last night nuzzled snug and sleeping with mom.

God is good. Thanks to everyone for your thoughts and prayers. FYI, the name Jake derives from the "pet name" origins of both John and Jack—which in Hebrew means "God is gracious." A second common meaning for Jake is "supplanter" or "conqueror."

Jake's middle name—Tory—is of Scottish decent and is short for "victory." For me, there was no other name... God singled it out early. Jake Tory ties in rather neatly with my own given name, Neil John—with Neil meaning "champion."

Another funny bit of trivia is the overabundance of the number four yesterday. We arrived at the hospital at nursing station four. Elana's O.R. room was #4—and so, too, was her recovery room. During Elana's C-section, I was escorted down to Room #240 to wait. Baby Jake was born at 11:44, weighing 6 pounds, 10 ounces (10 minus 6 is?). Now, Elana's hospital room is #344. And finally, the number of letters in our baby's first and middle names—FOUR!

AN EPILOGUE
AND A PROLOGUE

Jake is one year old now, and I can't believe it. Time has flown by so fast. Elana and I made it through our first year of parenthood largely unscathed. With one year down, I'm not so worried about Jake's second and third years anymore. Yes, this year has been challenging—but, overall, it hasn't been so bad.

For me, fatherhood has been fun. Time-consuming, life-altering, and full of unexpected surprises—but still, mostly fun.

Our son Jake Tory is destined for great things, I have no doubt. And I look forward to the future—anxious to see what lies ahead. Will we have another child? I don't know. For now, Elana and I are content to pour all of our time, attention, and love into Jake.

Whatever the future holds, I feel like I've finally arrived at a place of contentment. Here I sit, age forty-one. Forty-one years of a life on crutches with bent legs. I have been shaped by my disability and struggles, sure, but I have also had a few victories, too. A rewarding career, a loving wife, a son—all of these things have changed me, made me a better person.

Elana made me become the man (and husband) I always wanted to be. I am also thankful to Elana for showing me the love of Jesus. Becoming a Christian after almost thirty-five years of life, that was a defining moment for me. God has transformed me. With each passing year, and every significant life event, God continues to reveal Himself more and show His faithfulness, goodness, and grace.

My faith journey hasn't been easy, though. As a Christian, I was definitely a late-bloomer. The road was, at times, bumpy and awkward and atypical. But I made it. God was there to light my path and I made it.

Without question, I have lived a very blessed life. I wonder what's around the next bend...?

God knows.

Be reassured, and just wait.

ODDS AND ENDS

A BEDTIME STORY

"Waiter! Waiter, come quick! There's a dinosaur in my soup!"

The waiter calmly approaches the man's table.

"Is there something wrong, monsieur?"

"Yes. There is a dinosaur in my soup. A dinosaur, mister waiter sir!"

"Pardon me, monsieur—but I should think not."

"Oh, but there is. Honestly there is!"

"*Really,* monsieur! I must insist that you not waste my time like this…"

"And *I* insist that you inspect my soup."

A long pause, followed by a deep breath and slow exhale.

"Oh very well, monsieur. But I must ask you…"

The waiter pauses, grinning from ear to ear. A very tight grin.

"…I must ask you, what kind of soup *did* you order?"

"Why, mister waiter sir—can't you *tell?* It's tomato, of course."

"I believe you're right. Yes—yes, indeed it is. I am quite sure of it."

Another long pause.

"*Well?!*" says the diner.

"Yes…?" the waiter asks.

"Aren't you going to inspect my soup?"

"Oh, pardon me! Yes—yes, of course. Indeed I will. I will indeed! But first—oh forgive me for asking, but I am quite stupid in these matters and well, well…"

Yet another pause. Again grinning.

"Come on, out with it! What did you want to ask me, mister waiter sir?"

"Yes, well—isn't it… Sorry, what I *mean* to say is this… is it not customary for all orders of tomato soup to come with a dinosaur on the side?"

"Are you quite *serious*? I must say that I was never made aware of this!" says the diner.

"Yes, well—no matter. Would you like me to fetch the dinosaur out of your bowl, monsieur?"

"Please. Kindly, do—Do!"

"Very well, monsieur."

The waiter takes a large spoon and dredges the bottom of the soup bowl with it.

"I am very sorry, monsieur, but your dinosaur seems to have fled," says the waiter.

"*What?* The dinosaur—is *gone?!* Impossible! He was in my bowl a minute ago…"

The man—the diner, that is—glances quickly around the restaurant.

"Hey wait! Wait, mister waiter sir! Where's my suit? He's made off with my tuxedo. There's a dinosaur in my suit!"

"Suit? What suit?" asks the waiter.

"I had an extra suit with me. Didn't you notice it? See, I was going to pick up my wife later. We were going to see *The Phantom of the Opera* tonight."

"Hold on, monsieur. Let me see if I have this straight. You say there is a dinosaur in your *suit?*"

"Yes."

"Your *SUIT?*

"Yes!"

"Not soup? You didn't say *soup?*"

"No! I mean—yes, I *did,* but…"

The waiter interrupts.

"I am sorry, monsieur. I cannot help you."

The waiter turns back, and the diner can see that he is about to be left alone in his predicament. Having to act fast, he strips a Band-Aid off one of his fingers and tosses it into his bowl of soup.

"Uh, excuse me, mister waiter sir!"

The waiter turns to face the man.

"Yes, monsieur?"

"Aren't you going to bring me another bowl of tomato soup?"

"Why? The one you have is perfectly fine."

"But I told you—there's a diner's sore in this one!"

"I have already inspected the contents of your bowl. And I assure you—your dinosaur has fled."

"Uh, no. Perhaps you didn't hear me correctly. I said, *'diner's sore'.*"

"Yes—I know all about your dinosaur, monsieur."

"No, no! Not *'dinosaur'*—*'DINER'S sore'!*"

"I am afraid you have lost me, monsieur."

"Look here…" says the diner.

The waiter peers into the man's bowl of soup.

"Now—what's this, mister waiter sir?"

"Why, that looks like some small bandage of a sort."

"Exactly. And see that bit of dried blood there? See that? From one of the other diners, no doubt!"

"Uh, pardon me, monsieur. But what does all of this have to do with that dinosaur of yours?"

The diner's last ditch effort to save face had not worked. Still floating around in a bowl of tomato soup, the dinosaur saw everything. Handsomely attired in the tuxedo, he remained cleverly hidden under the guise of a soggy soda cracker.

A POEM FOR MOMMY
(A Celebration of the First Twelve Months)

I like how my mommy holds me,
comforts me. I like how she can soothe me
for all the times when I am restless and overtired.
The times when I miss my nap, the late nights,
the early mornings. Mommy is so patient with me!

And I like Mommy's soft voice
and the way she sings to me so sweetly.
Her voice is so gentle,
so calm. Always.

My mommy's a little different because she needs some help
to help care for me sometimes, but that's okay.
What Mommy can do,
she does—and I like it the best.

Mommy is so fun and engaging,
she makes me smile and laugh a lot.
I am so happy to have a mommy that cares for me
as much as she does. And usually so good at figuring out what
I want and need too—be it food, a diaper change, or a cuddle.

I love the way my mommy loves me
and I love my mommy.

FROM JAKE
(with a little help from Daddy)

THE SIN AND TEMPTATION OF YOUTH

I like the way
spat
toothpaste
foams up in the sink
all soft and silky and
I like the way
flowers
stink and
the way sceptics think and
goldfish drink and
I like the way you toss your hair
(yeah)
I like the way flowers stink.

IN TRANSIT

On the bus, she sits
looking out at the street
as houses, cars and trees pass by her window; they approach,
meet
and are gone.

A smile, soft and subtle,
drifts lazily across her face.
Like that of a dreamer
in thought suspended.

LOVE KNOT / LOVE NOT

Her head lies
on her pillow.
Lies heavy
and burdened
in a pillow cave,
smashed.

Lying
in such a way as to
tattoo slight linen creases on her left cheek.

She blinks at the harsh sun
seeping through pores in the curtain.
Knowing that the dream she has awoken from was somehow
easier.

Her eyes are cloudy,
like ocean water along a sandy beach.
The waves rolling in and out,
creating little storms beneath.
Disturbing a thousand grains of rock
and debris.

MOTIF

I.

The city falls under a black canopy. Cars scurry to and fro as the pelting rain bounces off roofs, windshields, and pavement. A parade of refracted light, white and red. Across the street, a fast-food restaurant; flashings of neon streak through the pounding sheets of water.

II.

The large lake is unsettled. A stiff wind stirs up whitecaps, they rise and fall. Along its shores, thick messes of long grass jet outward and thin skims of brown sludge float on the surface. Across the lake, on the horizon, a highway carved out of blasted rock twists aimlessly amongst the barren hills; an occasional tree clinging to the rock, desperate and grim-faced.

MODERN-DAY MEAL PREP

In the 19th century, hamburgers were often purely accidental.
A runaway plough versus a Jersey cow, for instance.
Nowadays,
things are a lot more purposeful –
a lot more manufactured.

Slow cows. Fast food.

Progress moves quicker still.

DEFINITION IN THE REAR-VIEW MIRROR
(Eye Exam Required)

E ran O it Cid
ver
Y
E ran O it Cid
ver
Y
E ran O it Cid

UH-OH CANADA

Sometimes, Canada—with its ten provinces and three territories—is seen
only as a marriage of convenience. On the whole, we Canadians in general
lack that fierce patriotism of our neighbours to the south.

As such, our country is a fragmented union held together by tree sap
and hockey tape.

But I love it anyway.

I do.

POLITICAL CORRECTNESS

One step forward, two steps back.
The inherent fault of political correctness.
A fatal flaw.
And yet most do not want to see it or admit to it.
Influential people,
past and present,
have turned a blind eye to it.

Sometimes, the pendulum swings too far in one direction.
Those who insist on being politically correct
are trying too hard. Trying too hard to single out visible
minorities
and fringe populations.

Political correctness is now just a backwards form of
segregation.
In striving for an ultimate fairness, political correctness is
most often
crumbling under all of its own weights and measures.

Legislative fairness and
self-imposed segregation does not always work the way it was
intended.

Let's try something else.

FOR MY WIFE, CHRISTMAS 2005

Your dark wavy hair is like the long silk ribbon; your soft lips like a big red bow.
An attached note, inked with words of love flows from your tongue; is reflected in your eyes. Your skin is the delicate pretty wrapping hiding a beautiful soul.

The perfect gift that I don't want to share with anyone.

JULY 12, 2006
(Reflecting Back on Three Years of Marriage)

My dearest Elana -
You are my best friend,
my lover,
my confidante and my cheerleader.

You are my nurturer, my pit-bull, and my daily fun.
You are my surprise; my something to look forward to.

Thanks to you and to God for my best three years so far. I
look forward to many, many more. One after another,
built upon all that is something really good.

VALENTINE'S DAY 2008
(For Mommy-to-Be)

First comes love,
then comes marriage...

And now, here comes our baby.

But in the beginning, love came first.

First comes love.

My love to you
and yours for me.

Love first. Always.

WRITERS BLOCK

My muse is mute,
my creativity spent and
I do not know where it all went.

My brain is sore,
my fingers permanently bent
from typing all day on my word processor.

And what place is this…? What this author calls "stuck"?

I am not sure.

Though perhaps, with luck,

THE END

about the author

Neil Matheson is a first-time writer from western Canada, currently residing in Surrey, British Columbia (near the outskirts of Vancouver).

Born on March 25, 1968, Mr. Matheson entered the world with a physical disability called Cerebral Palsy. From that day forward, Neil experienced life on a pair of crutches; walked through life on a pair of bent legs.

Despite his physical handicap, Neil grew up like any regular kid. And while not raised in a Christian home per se, Neil did manage to reach adulthood with at least some understanding of who God is.

Now, at forty-one years of age, the author reflects back on his life story. A journey on crutches: struggle, triumph, acceptance, love, and salvation... all retold here within the pages of this book.